Helping Baby Talk

"At last! An alternative to flash cards and rote language drills. HELPING BABY TALK tells parents what they can do *with* their child to stimulate language learning. The message to parents is clear: Talk with your baby about what interests them and understand how a child's language evolves. This informative book will guide parents' responses to their child from their baby's first babble to pre-schooler's conversation."

Dr. Susan Seidman
Developmental Psychologist
Rockland Childrens Psychiatric Center

"Thanks to HELPING BABY TALK, parents now have clear access to one of the most important aspects of their child's development. Not only do we learn that babies are expert communicators, but the wealth of fascinating research on language development also confirms that parents are their babies' best teachers. Besides being highly informative, this book is full of wonderful games to play and, more, is fun to read."

Frances Wells Burck
Author of *Babysense* and *Mothers Talking*

Helping Baby Talk

A Pressure-free Approach to Your Child's First Words from Birth to 3 Years

LORRAINE ROCISSANO, Ph.D.
AND
JEAN GRASSO FITZPATRICK

A SKYLIGHT PRESS BOOK

AVON BOOKS ◆ NEW YORK

HELPING BABY TALK is an original publication of Avon Books. This work has never before appeared in book form.

AVON BOOKS
A division of
The Hearst Corporation
105 Madison Avenue
New York, New York 10016

First Avon Books Printing: March 1990

AVON TRADEMARK REG. U.S. PAT. OFF. AND IN OTHER COUNTRIES, MARCA REGISTRADA, HECHO EN U.S.A.

Printed in the U.S.A.

RA 10 9 8 7 6 5 4 3 2 1

ACKNOWLEDGMENTS

The authors would like to thank Dr. Leslie Rescorla of Bryn Mawr College and Dr. Elizabeth Schnur of Harlem Hospital Center for their helpful suggestions on how to improve the manuscript. We also owe thanks to the many parents whose generous sharing of questions, concerns, and insights about their children's language development contributed to these pages. Meg Schneider and Lynn Sonberg of Skylight Press had the original idea for the book. Finally, thanks to the writers of the Hudson Group for camaraderie and advice, and to our families for their patience, and especially to our children, for their inspiration.

CONTENTS

FOREWORD

by Leslie Rescorla, Ph.D.,
Bryn Mawr College

Learning to talk is one of life's remarkable accomplishments. In the time period of just a few years, young children master the incredibly complex task of learning to speak and to understand their native language. Language is a universal human capacity. It seems to develop naturally and effortlessly in young children, whether they are rich or poor, whether they have many siblings or none, and whether they are learning English or Chinese. In *Helping Baby Talk*, Lorraine Rocissano and Jean Fitzpatrick have written a parents' guide to language acquisition which traces this remarkable learning process in a clear and vivid way.

One of the most important aspects of this book is its strong emphasis on language as a mode of social communication. The authors trace the origins of language to the child's earliest forms of social interaction; for instance, they show how young infants communicate with their caretakers by facial expression, sounds and noises, and body posture. Throughout their excellent account of the stages of language learning, the authors stress that children learn to speak because they want to share their ideas, perceptions, and feelings with the people who care for them. The authors do a nice job of describing some of the bad habits parents can fall into when they forget this basic communicative function of language— such as repeatedly "testing" their child's vocabulary, systematically withholding desired "goodies" until the child produces the correct phrase, or deliberately pretending not to comprehend when the child doesn't articulate clearly.

Helping Baby Talk helps parents learn more about language development in the context of the child's overall social, emotional, motor, and cognitive development. One of the nice features of the book is its smooth integration of a wealth of research and theory in child development, with many practical and concrete illustrations drawn from the authors' experience with real children and their parents. The careful reader of this book will learn about some of the classic literature in developmental psychology (for example, Piaget's work on sensory-motor intelligence, or Mahler's theory of separation-individuation in toddlers), as well as finding a clear presentation of much new and exciting contemporary research (Stern's work on mother-infant interaction, Kagan's account of the development of awareness of "standards" in the second year, or Izard's theory of the basic human emotions as manifested in facial expression). Research findings on infant visual and auditory perception and on motor development are woven into the book to give parents a context for the unfolding of language acquisition.

This book combines a thorough and sophisticated presentation of the current research in language acquisition with a multitude of colorful anecdotes, practical advice, and cautionary suggestions. Parents will learn a great deal about the stages of early babbling (from coos to "papa"), about "overextension" of early vocabulary words (e.g., calling all animals "doggie"), about the characteristics of "telegraphic speech" (as in, "me want cookie"), and about the overregularization of grammatical inflections (as in, "they flied away" or "let's feed the gooses"). They will also discover that the book contains an abundance of "helpful hints" which Dr. Rocissano has found to be effective in her work with parents and their young children—suggestions for activities parents can do with children to foster healthy language development, tips on handling children's language "errors," and even a list of eight strategies for coping with a colicky infant!

In this age of fast-paced, high-pressured living, there are many books on the market aimed at telling parents how to make their infant "smarter," how to give their child a head start on the "fast track to success." In *Helping Baby Talk*, Rocissano and Fitzpatrick explicitly and emphatically reject this goal. They present language as a natural developmental capacity which evolves within the context of social interaction and interpersonal communication. They argue convincingly that "hurrying" young children to talk (such as "force-feeding" vocabulary so that Jimmy will be the first child in the playgroup to have 50 words) has no beneficial effect on long-term language skill, and can in fact be harmful. For example, children who feel pressured to talk often begin to regard language as a weapon which they can use to assert their autonomy and express their resistance. This distorts the natural desire young children have to communicate, and may actually retard language acquisition.

Parents reading *Helping Baby Talk* will find that it enhances their appreciation and acceptance of their own child. The authors write eloquently of the importance of being sensitive to the cues a baby gives, of "fine-tuning" stimulation to "fit" with the infant's style. Rocissano and Fitzpatrick also stress the importance of listening to what the child is trying to say and being responsive to his or her communications, however imperfectly they are expressed. The authors highlight the importance of using language to focus on the topics and events which the child is interested in, noting that a toddler is much more likely to learn words which refer to things he or she is fascinated by (like cars or dogs), than words which might be high on a parent's agenda (like color names).

In conclusion, *Helping Baby Talk* is a highly entertaining and very informative book about language development in young children. The authors have achieved an admirable integration of research findings, colorful examples, sound advice, and helpful suggestions. Parents will find that the book increases their information about the remarkable process of language learning, provides them with a wealth of practical suggestions about activities they can do with a young child, and reminds them that language is first and foremost the medium of social communication between individuals who care about one another and respect each other's individuality.

ONE

Letting Language Happen

It's hard to imagine any aspect of a child's growth that is more delightful than the development of language. From the crying baby to the babbling one-year-old, the child seems to blossom almost overnight into a preschooler who asks questions that have been puzzling great minds throughout the ages—anything from "Why are there trees?" to "Why don't I ever get what I want?" Long before he says his first word, he is making enormous strides in his ability to communicate and to understand what others are saying. Recognizing these signs of language growth is not always easy—especially during the first year of life. You've probably heard people make remarks like, "Babies are pretty boring until they're six months old, because up until then you can't really communicate with them." Well, that depends on what you mean by *communicate*. There's no question that if you think

3

of communication as speech, you're going to find your child's first year of life rather unexciting, and perhaps even discouraging.

But understanding the process of early language development can be a real eye-opener, as we've both frequently discovered in our professional lives—as a developmental psychologist in private practice who leads educational groups for parents of young children, and as a professional child-development writer. Whether parents are concerned about language or any other aspect of development, they often ask questions about what is "normal"—and what is not—during these crucial early years. It is gratifying to see the change that can occur when one such worried or bewildered parent receives accurate information about child development: often, she becomes a confident parent, and even an excited one. Likewise, when you learn to recognize the many different ways your child communicates, you'll be amazed at how much he actually "says."

In this book we present many of the steps in a baby's developing communication—steps that (though often little-noticed) demonstrate, as surely as the first word, that your baby is moving along the road to language use. We offer a stage-by-stage guide to a child's language development and linguistic "milestones" from birth to three years. Obviously, this growth does not occur in isolation; language development is inextricably linked with your baby's progress in other areas. For this reason, each stage of language growth described in these pages is viewed in the broader context of the child's unfolding social skills, motor coordination, and intellectual abilities. Likewise, our advice on how to foster your child's language growth does not focus on turning your baby into an early talker, but instead on addressing the needs of the whole child. You will find many real-life examples of young children's early communication attempts, with reassuring explanations of the most common errors children make and how to handle them. There is plenty of practical, down-to-earth advice on helping your child's language grow—without turning yourself into a language "coach." And in special boxes highlighted in each chapter, we suggest a wide variety of simple, language-enriching activities that can easily become enjoyable parts of your daily routine.

As you will see, there is no reason to prod or push your child into language. In this book—which is based on more than ten years of research in children's language development and work with hundreds of children and parents in child-development laboratory settings, as well as on our firsthand experiences as mothers of young children—we want to assure you that learning to speak comes as naturally to a young child as learning to walk or to play. Your baby will be your willing partner in the exciting adventure of learning to communicate. The more you know about the fascinating process by which children learn to speak, the more confident you will feel letting your child's language abilities joyfully and spontaneously unfold as nature intended.

Fun, Not Flash Cards

Like all human beings, young children love to talk about what they're doing and thinking, but they're especially fond of chatting about the things they come to know through hands-on experience, from block towers to mud pies. For this reason, this book does not offer a method designed to create pint-size linguistic geniuses—by having children simply parrot words after someone else's cues, for instance, or recite the names of objects on flash cards. This is *not* a step-by-step guide in how to teach your baby to talk. In fact, that's exactly the kind of book we've taken great pains to avoid writing. The things most of us do naturally—playing peekaboo while changing a diaper, asking a toddler whether he wants a cracker with his apple juice, or talking with a three-year-old about taking turns during a play date—all contribute far more than we realize to a child's growing ability to understand and use language. Babies do learn to talk from the adults around them, but it's through natural, day-to-day activities and interactions. They simply don't seem to learn to talk through a series of formal lessons and, in fact, such lessons can not only be ineffective but harmful. Force-feeding language to babies and young children dampens motivation and may do lasting harm to the relationship between parent and child.

One mother, for example, was upset that her two-and-a-half-year-old son, James, seemed to refuse to speak to her, even though she knew he could say about ten words. It wasn't hard to figure out why young James had stopped talking to his mother; her idea of dialogue was a series of drills. Talk was for teaching. No matter how indifferent little James appeared, he needed to learn certain Very Important Lessons—the names of colors, for instance. Cheerfully James' mom would hold up cups in varying hues and expect him to repeat: "Green! Red! Blue!" No wonder James refused to cooperate with her. She rarely responded with more than a perfunctory "Yes, that's a truck," when James pointed to one, and hardly ever tried to engage him in conversation about the toys with which he was playing. It was no surprise that James' language skills were lagging behind those of most children of his age.

Sometimes it is tempting to institute a mini-language program, and become a coach, because we are measuring our child against the nearest available yardstick—either a milestone chart or our next-door neighbor's baby album. In our competitive culture, new parents are often fraught with anxiety if their children aren't among the first on the playground to attain new skills. That goes double for language, perhaps because our information-based society offers such rich rewards to "smooth talkers," from sales representatives to TV newscasters. If you fear that your child will end up at the bottom of his class if his language develops at a slower rate than that of his friends, it's easy to fall into the trap of trying to "help him along a little."

Two-year-old Sam, for example, was extremely reluctant to ask for things in words. Why, Sam's parents wondered, had he not turned out to be an early talker despite their concerted efforts? They had gone to great pains to spur his language development by "forcing him" to use language. They refused to give him anything he wanted unless he asked for it correctly, offering "rewards for words." If Sam "asked" for a cookie by pointing and vocalizing, his mother kept the lid on the cookie jar until he pronounced the word *cookie*. Sam would resist and resist until finally, out of sheer desperation, he'd blurt out the word, almost choking on it in the process. What his mother had done by insisting on the use of words from an early age was to alter the natural pattern of unfolding communication. She had disturbed what would have been his natural desire to speak when he was ready. And in fact, she had made talking a very unpleasant experience for her child—one he did his best to avoid.

Unfortunately, milestone charts and developmental schedules that have been adapted from professional child-development literature often seem to cause parents unnecessary concern and, at times, even seem to alarm them into embarking on misguided "catch-up" campaigns similar to that adopted by Sam's mother. For this reason, we've been careful to address the concerns that many parents have about what constitutes a "normal" rate of language development. In each chapter we provide age *ranges* in normal children for every linguistic milestone introduced in this book. There is *no* evidence to show that a child who is the first to develop a new language skill necessarily maintains his advantage as time goes by. Just as the earliest walker is not guaranteed to grow up and win the Boston Marathon, the early talker doesn't necessarily grow up to be a Shakespearean actor. And in fact, many "slow" talkers catch up long before adulthood. One small boy, for example, who apparently saw no need to utter more than a few words even at twenty-two months, was singled out at the age of two and a half by his nursery school teacher as "one of our best talkers." A child's early or late speech is not a reliable indicator of intelligence; after all, Einstein himself was reputed to be a very late talker. Just as achieving a milestone early is not necessarily a sign of special ability, reaching a milestone late is no guarantee of *lack* of ability.

In order to help your child's language blossom, you need to learn to be sensitive to his own unique approach to verbal expression, and to cultivate an awareness of the moods and interests that will play such an important part in his attempts to learn to communicate. Hard-and-fast rules are no help in this complex, highly individual process, because each child's language develops differently. The most important thing you can do is to *follow your child's lead.* Notice what your child is interested in, and talk with him about that. As he grows more and more confident of his communication skills—and continues to trust that you are genuinely interested in what he has to say—he will learn to use language in ways that are increasingly complex and expressive.

Talking and Temperament

Few people realize how much a child's *temperament*, or personality style, influences the way he learns to talk. It's important to keep in mind that not only does the *rate* of speech development vary considerably from one child to another, but that there are many different *styles* of communication as well. This shouldn't come as too much of a surprise when you consider the variety of adult modes of speech—compare, say, a disc jockey on a New York Top 40 radio station with a Trappist monk!

Recent research suggests that these personality differences between people are *not* determined exclusively by upbringing. In their pioneering work the psychiatrists Alexander Thomas and Stella Chess of New York University Medical Center have confirmed something parents have long suspected—that there seems to be a constitutional component, usually called "temperament," in even the tiniest infants. For example, some babies tend to approach new experiences with great gusto, enthusiasm, and excitement, while others are easily overwhelmed. Some babies thrive on social experiences, enjoying new people and large groups, while others stay on the sidelines or cling to Mommy or Daddy's leg. Some

babies seem to be born with sunny disposi-
tions and a smile on their faces, while others
are "full of woe," cranky and hard to please.

When it comes to language, some young
children take such delight in their growing
ability to speak that they turn into real chat-
terboxes. "By the time my son was two and a
half," one mother recalls, "we used to set the
kitchen timer for fifteen seconds and tell him,
'No talking until the buzzer goes off,' just so
we'd have a chance to hear ourselves think!"
By the same token, a perfectly normal child
the same age may be the "silent type," who
only talks when necessary and needs some
time (and a patient listener) to formulate what
he wants to say. While your home environment will certainly play a role in your child's
language style, it's important to acknowledge
and respect his own inclinations.

Partners in Communication

There's one more reason we are not offering detailed instructions on how to teach
your baby to talk, and that is because *no one*
knows as well as you do what your child
needs most. When it comes to your baby,
you're the expert. That's not only because
you spend a great deal of time with your
child, but because you play a role in his life

and development that no one else can. Language learning is very much a part of the unique *relationship* between you and your child. And as in any relationship, that means a give-and-take. Babies are not passive receptacles which adults fill with words; they are *partners in communication.* Far from being the "blank slates" philosophers and psychologists once assumed them to be, even the tiniest babies can participate in nonverbal "conversation," as anyone who's ever enjoyed a cooing session with an infant well knows.

Sadly, when parents decide to use an "expert" method of "teaching" communication instead of encouraging their child's language learning in the context of the family's everyday, loving relationship, they are invariably disappointed with the results. Jane, whose daughter Allison was two, had read in a magazine article that the best way to motivate her child to speak was to offer lavish praise for every spoken word. She was particularly fond of "fill-in-the-blank" games (Mom: "What does the cow say?" Child: "Moo." Mother, clapping: "Right! That's wonderful! What a smart girl Allison is!"). Unfortunately, the method backfired. It didn't take long for Allison to discover that Mommy was the only person around who was such an appreciative audience, and she refused to talk to anyone except Jane. While there's nothing wrong with praising your child's developing speech, turning conversation into a test of perfor- mance only stifles his natural tendency to express himself in words.

How much more rewarding it is to en- courage your child's language learning by responding to him spontaneously and natu- rally! Your baby is motivated to learn not only to get his needs met but also out of the sheer joy of sharing his exciting new discoveries of the world around him. One ten-month-old, for example, discovered his reflection in a full-length mirror and shrieked the news to his mother: "Eeeh! Eeeh!" And a twenty-two-month-old girl put on a new— and slightly oversize—dress for the first time, looked down at its ankle-length skirt, tossed her blonde ringlets, and exclaimed, "*I'm* a ballerina!" These precious moments are matchless opportunities for you as a parent to take a fresh look at life from a child's perspective, and to let your child dis- cover how gratifying it is to share his thoughts with someone who cares enough to really listen.

What's Ahead

You'll find it easy to follow your child's language development with this book. The chapters are arranged chronologically, beginning with the newborn. Each chapter is devoted to a specific period of development. As we've already mentioned, because language learning is an inextricable part of your child's overall physical, emotional, and social growth, we've included a developmental "portrait" of sorts under the heading "Growing and Changing: The Context for Communication" in each chapter. Following is a section titled "Language Learning Now," which provides helpful information for parents on how communication develops. Next comes "Everyday Language Learning: How to Help," a comprehensive guide to fostering your child's communication within the context of everyday life, from dinnertime to day care to diaper changes. (This section will also take note of some of the classic habits many parents and caregivers fall into which can create problems in the long run.) Supplementing the practical advice in this section are special boxes highlighting language-enriching activities caregivers and children can enjoy together in the context of daily life. Each chapter concludes with a section entitled "Questions Parents Ask . . ." which includes questions and problems posed by real-life parents and offering concise, practical answers based on current research. We hope that this book will serve not as the basis of a "language curriculum" for your child, but as a reassuring guide to help you discover your baby's own unique approach to communication and *enjoy* it for all its exuberance and freshness.

***

TWO

Birth to Two Months: First Connections

Holding a new baby for the first time, many a parent is a little surprised and even slightly disappointed. Where is the plump, smiling baby we expected? In fact, she's rather thin, and her expression is often vague. As for communication, at first it's about as clear as a long-distance phone call during a thunderstorm: the baby spends much of *her* time crying, and we spend most of *ours* trying to figure out why. At moments when there is a meeting of the minds—when she sighs blissfully after a loudly demanded extra feeding, for example—it's gratifying to realize we are growing to understand one another. This is primarily a time for you and your baby to recover from the birth trauma, to adjust to life as a new family, and to enjoy the physical contact that, for now, is your most important means of communication. In these early days you and your baby will "talk" through touch.

Much as we'll welcome the day when we hear her murmur, "I love you, Mommy," at this stage skin-to-skin contact is our primary means of expressing our love and caring. For now we can take pleasure in the tiny hands that grasp our fingers, or the mouth that seeks the nipple and sucks eagerly. The newborn period is a precious time to begin to understand what your baby is trying to tell you, and to catch some exciting glimpses of the social creature she'll soon become.

While many parents enjoy these fleeting days, others find it hard to have strong feelings of love toward their baby until a month or so later, when she can make real eye contact and give a gummy smile. As one new father remarked affectionately, his baby son was certainly cute and cuddly, but the family dog (who recognized at least ten words, including "walk" and "dinner") was way ahead of Michael in the communication department at this stage!

During the first few weeks of life your baby is still coping with the enormous adjustment of living outside the womb, with her own body now controlling vital functions (such as respiration, temperature control, eating, and excreting) that were until recently performed for her, through the umbilical cord. You might think of her, as one mother put it, as "awakening from the long fetal sleep." Right now what she needs most is a calm environment in which to gradually "awaken." After all, think of all the new ways her senses are being stimulated by the world outside the womb. She feels air brushing past her cheek, she gets too hot (or too cold), she sucks and tastes the warmth and sweetness of milk. Your baby can also hear all sorts of noises—from the chirping of birds to television commercials to the washing machine. All of this is quite enough to occupy her for the time being.

For all these reasons, there is no need to expose your baby to a blitz of additional stimuli during these early weeks. Your baby is not quite ready for the kind of extended give-and-take that adults tend to think of as communication. But without even realizing it you have probably already begun communicating in ways she finds very appealing. Right from the start most of us tend to instinctively begin talking to our babies, even though we know they won't answer back. We speak in high voices, slowly and soothingly. Do you ever wonder what other people would think if they heard you chattering away ("And now Daddy's going to put Laura's baby toes into the nice bootie . . .")? Well, rest assured that your baby loves every minute. In fact, we now know that babies are actually able to take advantage of their parents' natural desire to have "conversations" with them. Long before they're able to even gurgle or coo, they're quietly learning about their world and the special

people in it. And hearing isn't the only sense
that's been underrated. While even our parents thought babies were blind at birth as well
as unable to feel pain, taste, or smell, recent
research shows how wrong they were. Newborns have sensory systems that, though still
immature by adult standards, are anything
but useless. From birth a baby's senses are
well-attuned to take in all the sights and
sounds to which she will be exposed. The result? Within two or three months, she turns
into the real communication partner you were
expecting all along!

Growing and Changing: The Context for Communication

One of the biggest limitations on communication development at this stage is the fact
that most of the time, your newborn baby
isn't alert enough to listen to you talk or even
focus on your face. New babies usually sleep
a lot. During the first few weeks, most of them
will sleep as much as sixteen to seventeen
hours a day, cycling in and out of sleep and
awakening for a feeding every two to four
hours.

When newborns are awake, that usually

means something different than it does for the rest of us. We adults tend to think of being awake as a time when we're bright-eyed and ready for activity of one sort or another. But new babies are only alert that way for very brief periods. Most of their movements are still *reflexive,* which means that they are automatic responses to specific kinds of stimulation—*rooting,* or turning her head toward a touch on her cheek and searching with her mouth, and *sucking* on a nipple to take in liquid. During most of their waking time, they tend to be glassy-eyed or drowsy. When you see your baby looking this way, that's a good sign she'd like some quiet time. A drowsy baby is not responsive to interaction with a parent or caregiver. She is not even ready to take in the sounds and sights of a stroller ride through the mall, or to enjoy lively music on the radio. Such an intensive "program" may merely inspire her to drift off to sleep. If you push her too far, she may grow cranky and be hard to soothe.

Even when she's alert, you may notice that your baby is busy kicking and waving her arms, or just plain fussy. As you've no doubt concluded, when that happens she's alert but unhappy, usually because she's hungry, tired, wet, or overstimulated. These aren't moments when she's ready to take in the world around her, either. The state of quiet alertness, when her eyes are bright and focused and she *is* ready to "tune in" to your conversation or look at her new rattle, doesn't appear too frequently at this stage. You're most likely to notice it when your baby is feeling very contented and comfortable, especially after a feeding (unless she falls asleep) or a nap.

Making Sense of the World

An infant can *see* from the moment of birth. Her visual system is far from fully mature, of course, but an infant can see much more than simple light and shadow. She has a maximum focus range of about eight to twelve inches (making her rather near sighted), and she can see anything that distance from her eyes—your face, say, or a rattle. Move further away and the image gets blurry, as it does for a nearsighted adult, but the baby can still see shapes and movement all the way across a room.

During those brief moments when young babies are in an alert state, they give clear signs that they *want* to see the world around them. Professor Jerome Bruner and his colleagues at Harvard University found that as early as five or six weeks of age babies will suck harder on a specially wired pacifier to bring a fuzzy picture into focus. We also know that babies are more attracted to some things than to others. For one thing, young infants would rather look at a familiar object—such as a picture on the nursery wall—than at a strange one. This isn't too surprising, when you consider that to a newborn the world is almost entirely strange. It must give baby a sense of security and comfort to see something that looks familiar now and then! (By three months or so, however, she starts to prefer novel sights to familiar ones.)

Movement also attracts baby's attention. Even a newborn can focus on and follow or *track* a slowly moving object such as a crib mobile. Some researchers think infants can see color, and that red and blue are particular favorites among newborns. One mother told us that one of the few ways to soothe her colicky baby in the evenings was to put him on his changing table, where he would stare intently at the red pipes running across the ceiling!

Baby's *hearing* develops earlier than you might suspect—by one month before birth, when they hear sounds from Mom's heartbeat to Daddy's voice outside the womb. At birth, babies can distinguish between sounds that are familiar (those they've been hearing while in utero) and those that are new to them. Research done on slightly older babies has shown that infants also respond faster to a new speech sound after getting bored by an old speech sound. This seems to indicate that the infant is preadapted, or naturally equipped, to perceive certain fine distinctions in human speech. Of course, babies this age don't yet understand that these different sounds *mean* anything. It will take many months of hearing language and how it is used in the world before your baby begins to understand how sound and meaning are related.

A Social Creature

Have you noticed how interested your baby is in your *face*? When new babies look at faces, they seem to be especially attracted to the boundaries, such as the hairline and chin. But by one month of age, they begin to look at features—especially eyes. That means you can look forward to eye contact with your baby, which is not only an important aspect of communication between people at every age but an exciting indication that, in one father's words, "we're getting through the fog." Studies also show that even a newborn finds a live person's face more intriguing than a photograph and will scrutinize it far more intently than she will a picture. In fact, researchers have found that infants often become upset when presented with a live, impassive face.

As we've mentioned, our baby's ability to make and sustain *eye contact* with us is an important communication milestone. Selma Fraiberg, a psychoanalyst and author of the classic *The Magic Years*, believed that eye contact is a universal human signal that we're ready for interaction. She found that parents of blind infants actually tended to feel rejected because of their babies' inability to make eye contact. Even with a normal newborn, eye contact is rare, and this may make it hard to feel that we're "getting through." Don't be surprised if you feel discouraged and even unappreciated in these early weeks.

You may find yourself wondering whether she sees or hears *you* as Mommy or Daddy. Does she have any idea who you are? Can she appreciate all your efforts to communicate—the loving "Good morning, precious" you manage even after a nearly sleepless night? Parenting a new baby, who cannot yet give us the eye contact or the smiles we so long for, requires us to rely heavily on faith—that the baby will come to understand us much better when she is more mature. In the meantime, skin-to-skin contact with her (more on this below) is the way to say, "I love you" to a newborn or young infant. Within two months, you'll be gazing into each other's eyes more and more often, and feel yourself amply rewarded with the gift of your baby's glowing smile!

The social readiness with which your baby is born is also revealed by the kinds of *sounds* she likes to hear. Researchers have recently discovered that newborns are actually born with preferences for certain kinds of sounds— high-pitched voices, for example, which is why the seemingly silly falsetto we use when we talk to babies is just right. And although we might expect that babies would love the sounds of our favorite music, they actually prefer another universal sound—that of human talk. What's more, a newborn baby will often turn toward her mother when she hears her speak, a sign of recognition that precedes the social smile and can be *very* gratifying to Mom if she notices it. Research shows that baby has grown familiar with her mother's voice during her sojourn in the womb! As for Dad, his voice is clearly favored over those of other males after baby is several weeks of age.

Your newborn expresses her sociability by the way she *moves* when you look at her or talk to her. The well-known pediatrician T. Berry Brazelton discovered that two-week-old babies move differently, for example, depending on whether they're looking at their mothers or a stationary object. Looking at an interesting toy, the baby seems to strain toward it with her whole body. Her expression is fixed, with little animation, and she seems to be concentrating intently. Looking at Mom, on the other hand, she responds to a smile or friendly word with a fascinating pattern of movement resembling a dance. First baby seems to strain toward her just as she does toward the toy, but then she draws in her arms and legs as if expecting Mom to approach. If you notice your baby doing this, you might be surprised at your *own* unconscious movements. According to Dr. Brazelton's study, most mothers follow along Ginger Rogers–style, moving toward baby as she moves back and then leaning back as baby advances.

At this stage, baby's progress may seem like a series of very tiny steps. But keep in mind that it's only recently that researchers have discovered how very much young babies do respond to *and affect* their social environment. Not long ago experts assumed that babies were influenced by the people around them but did little to contribute to their own social experiences. We now know that even newborns are preadapted to interpret all sorts of visual and auditory communication and have a rather impressive capacity to respond with a variety of facial expressions, gestures, and cries. This doesn't mean, of course, that baby is deliberately "trying to tell you something." Instead nature seems to have equipped baby with signals that adult caregivers are able to read as "I'm hungry," "I'm tired," and "I like being talked to," long before baby is able to say so. Keep in mind that for now baby's communication signals only "work" when parents or caregivers are alert to them and willing to respond—a stark contrast with those of, say, a two-year-old, who can endlessly whine, "I want you, Mommy." Fortunately, researchers have discovered that by and large parents naturally respond to their babies in ways that encourage them to communicate.

Language Learning Now

Crying

Just as baby's appearance isn't exactly what we expected, her vocalizations in these early weeks don't sound anything like the cooing and gurgling we'd anticipated. One new father commented that his newborn son's assorted sniffles, snorts, and grunts sounded "like a barnyard," and medical professionals usually describe them as "vegetative noises." Most of baby's early sounds have little communicative value. But *cries* are a conspicuous exception. Cries are certainly nowhere near as precise as words as means of communication, but they do sound different enough that most parents gradually learn to recognize their meanings. As usual when it comes to children's communication, each baby has her own style of crying, and no one knows as much about your child as you. But many parents do recognize different cries and begin to associate certain patterns with baby's demands. The *hunger* cry, for example, is often regular and rhythmic, while a baby in *pain* will usually let out one long wail or scream, followed by a gasp. (That plaintive wail strikes terror in the hearts of many a parent. It's no surprise that the psychologist Peter Wolff found in a classic study that mothers respond more quickly to cries of pain than to either hunger or anger cries.) Perhaps the hardest cry for a caregiver to listen to is the *fussiness* cry. Not that it's loud—it tends to be a mild whimper, but many babies can keep it up for hours, driving adults to distraction.

Perhaps what makes crying so frustrating is that it's a symptom of our basic communication problem with our baby. She simply can't explain herself in words, and the fussy cry is her only way of saying, "Something's bothering me!" Unfortunately, this doesn't tell us what's bothering her, and so the whimpering goes on. Keep in mind that crying differs from language not only in its volume and lack of precision, but also because it is not an *intentional* form of communication. Even though sometimes it may sound, in one new mother's words, as though your baby is saying, "How *dare* you treat me this way!" in reality a new baby does not make any logical connection between her crying and anyone's listening or coming to comfort her—although your attempts at soothing her are first steps in helping her learn to make that association. Once you're sure baby isn't hungry, tired, or bored, try one of the soothing techniques on pages 38–40. A change of scene may help distract your baby from crying. When nothing works, take comfort in the thought that some pediatricians suggest babies actually *need* fuss time to relieve tension before falling asleep. As your baby's nervous system matures she'll probably do less fussy crying and "progress" to cries of a more readable ilk.

Facial Expressions

If you pay attention, your baby's *facial expressions* can tell you a great deal. Long ago Charles Darwin noted that certain facial expressions are common in many cultures and seem to have universal meanings. A smile, for example, means very much the same thing to an Eskimo, a Bushman, and an Italian. Disgust (curled lips and wrinkled nose) is understood by everyone from Japan to Saudi Arabia. Likewise, we all know that lowered brows, narrowed eyes, flaring nostrils, and open mouth mean anger. Newborns, being youthful members of the human race, already produce some of these universal facial signals. Psychologist Carroll Izard and his colleagues at the University of Delaware studied how even newborns can express interest, distress, or disgust with their tiny faces. He had adults judge emotions expressed in photographs of infants, and found that most agreed about the emotion on each baby's face. Izard concluded that these emotional expressions are not only universal but inborn.

Babies are also experts in body language. When she's having fun, you may notice your infant quivering from head to toe. When she's angry she'll be all arms and legs flailing, body writhing, and fists tightly clenched. You can tell a lot about your baby's likes and dislikes from the way she moves. When she's interested in or curious about something, she will turn her head toward it, or even stick out her tongue! On the other hand, when she wants to avoid a scene or face out of boredom or overstimulation, she'll turn away. Have you occasionally noticed your baby arching her back and moving her head away? That's her way of saying, "I don't want to be social anymore—please don't talk to me or kiss me now, because I've had enough!"

Everyday Language Learning: How to Help

Building the Relationship

There's no baby in the world quite like yours. Even as early as the first few weeks of life babies differ from one another in very many ways, and communication style is no exception. This is an important time to begin to "tune in" to your baby, to become sensitive to the kinds of contact and interaction with which she seems most comfortable. Developing this kind of sensitivity is essential to any genuine relationship, and more than any particular words you say to your baby it is your relationship that is at the heart of communication development. Although her way of responding to the world around her in these early weeks may change with time (take heart, parents of colicky babies!), noticing some of her preferences now may offer clues to her temperament, which, as we shall see in later chapters, will affect her style of communicating as she grows older. One characteristic you will probably become aware of— and which can affect communication between you and your baby enormously—is something developmental experts call *sensory threshold*. What it refers to is how sensitive a

AND BELLS ON HER TOES . . .

As baby becomes more alert and active, between six and eight weeks, try attaching bells to her booties, or make a bell bracelet for her wrist by stringing a sleigh bell on a piece of elastic. She will enjoy the sound of the bells and slowly come to realize that her own action produces the noise.

baby is to a particular sensory stimulation, such as sound or touch. Is your baby one who loves to be jiggled and lifted high in the air, or does she prefer to be cradled quietly in your arms? Does she startle when someone sneezes or coughs nearby? Does she enjoy gazing at the bright ceiling lamp over the changing table, or prefer to look away or even close her eyes?

Noticing these preferences will help you understand what your baby's idea of a good time is—and what's likely to upset her. We have seen a doting grandfather, for example, grow frustrated and annoyed when his well-meaning attempts to play with his infant grandson left the baby upset and screaming. Before long, someone in the family realized that Grandad's booming voice was simply overwhelming young Jason. When the grandfather learned to speak in low tones, their fledgling relationship took a much more promising turn. Keep in mind that a baby who

is highly sensitive to touch may draw away
from cuddling or cry when held, not because
she dislikes people but because for her such
close touch is simply too intense. If your baby
is like this it can be hard not to feel rejected
sometimes. After all, aren't babies supposed
to be the world's all-time great cuddlers? But
instead of taking your baby's style personally,
why not try to find what she *does* find pleasurable. Maybe she enjoys looking at photos
of smiling faces, or likes to hear you chatter
or sing to her. As your child develops, you'll
continue to notice the special personality
characteristics that make your child the individual—sometimes wonderful, sometimes
frustrating—that she is. Learning to accept
her as a separate person with qualities and
quirks all her own is the first step in establishing good communication with your baby.

Respecting Baby's Mood

Accepting her as a separate person means
approaching the issues of language and communication with care and respect for your little one's needs and preferences. Don't worry
about the serious business of "maximizing
baby's preadaptive tendencies;" at this point
your baby will most appreciate your simple,
loving attempts to gauge her mood and readiness for stimulation. Before you bombard her

SKIN-TO-SKIN CONTACT

Your baby will enjoy any contact with you or the new world around her through her *senses*, especially touch, sight, or sound. Although some babies shy away from cuddling because they're extra-sensitive to it, the typical newborn is very eager to "get physical." Obviously breast-feeding is nature's way of building skin-to-skin contact into baby's routine, but Mom or Dad can hold baby close during a bottle feeding as well. One father whose baby was born in the summer enjoyed going shirtless every evening after work and holding baby in his arms. Dance cheek-to-cheek with your infant, lie on the floor with her resting on your chest, or laze in a hammock or in bed. When baby wants to be held and you need to get things done, try wearing her in a front carrier with neck support, such as a Snugli.

with a loud chorus of "This Old Man," consider whether baby appears to be in the state of quiet alertness we've discussed earlier in this chapter. Maybe a gentle rendition of "Rock-a-Bye Baby" is more suited to her. Only during those few minutes each day is she ready for anything as exciting as "conversation" with Mommy. When she looks drowsy, it's wise to respect her need for quiet or comforting.

Even tiny babies are expert communicators when it comes to complaining loudly. They can cry for hours, right? Unfortunately, since babies can't offer any details about what's wrong, if indeed anything is, parents are not infrequently left wondering whether they will *ever* figure out how to get them to stop. For those times, we offer this list of tips from mothers and fathers on how to soothe your endlessly crying baby:

- *Rapid rocking.* Like Whistler's mother, most of us are pretty sedate when we sit in a rocking chair. But strangely enough, *high-speed* rocking is actually more effective in calming a fussy baby. You might find it easier to sit in a regular chair (not a rocker) and hold your baby over your shoulder while you move your own body quickly back and forth, being careful to support baby's neck. Putting baby in a stroller, carriage, or infant seat and rocking quickly can also be effective.
- *Swaddling.* This age-old remedy, in which the baby is wrapped tightly to restrict the movements of her limbs, is often soothing—perhaps because it reminds her of the snugness of the womb! Infant carriers that hold baby tight and close to you—the Snugli type—are also calming to many babies.
- *Warm bath.* Particularly helpful when baby has gas, this is a good way to relax her muscles. Be sure her tummy is well underwater. You might also try having her lie on a *warm* hot-water bottle wrapped in a towel so

it won't burn (after filling, press the bottle to squeeze out the air before replacing the cap, or it won't feel warm).

- *Suspension in a blanket.* This method was recently suggested to us by two different mothers of colicky infants. You and your spouse (or another caretaker) each hold one end of the blanket with baby cradled in the middle, hammock-style. The sensation of being suspended in a dark, warm, womblike place can be very comforting. There is a commercial baby hammock available that you can put inside the crib.

- *Vibration.* Car rides are often comforting, but placing baby on top of the running washer or dryer is more convenient and may also calm baby. Naturally, a baby should *never* be left unattended in this position. There is even a new gadget on the market that attaches to baby's crib to produce a vibration similar to a car motor!

- *Heartbeats.* A clock ticking, a stuffed animal that plays a heartbeat, or a recording of "sounds from the womb" (featuring heartbeat and the rushing of blood through veins and arteries) can bring back fond memories for baby. We know some mothers who say music with a loud, steady beat—the kind played in aerobic dance classes—is more effective than the sweetest of lullabies.

- *Radio.* Since babies seem to like the sound of human voices, you might take a tip from one mother we know who played a low-key radio talk show in her baby's room. An "easy listening" station may also calm your baby—the mixture of soothing talk with soothing music is tailor-made to the diaper-clad listener! The radio is an ideal short-term companion for the baby who's fussy due to boredom.

- *Visual stimulation.* You can calm a bored baby by taking advantage of her interest in pattern and movement. Position the infant seat so that baby can watch you performing a household activity. Hang magazine pictures (preferably of faces—babies' and adults') near the changing table and the infant seat, and once baby seems interested in novel things (at three months or so) change them regularly to keep baby interested. Take the mobile off the crib and set it up where baby spends most of her day.

When all else fails, why not get some relief for *yourself?* Enlist your spouse, or a relative or a friend, to try comforting the baby while you take a break. If your baby has regular bouts of colic, consider hiring a teenager to come in and walk her back and forth for an hour every day. If another person has more luck than you in soothing the baby, don't take it personally or decide you're a bad parent. Anybody on round-the-clock duty gets tied up in knots after a while. Besides, young babies often quiet down when picked up by a stranger because they are focusing on the novelty of how they are being held. When you absolutely can't stand another minute, put the baby in the crib for a while and concentrate on relaxing: try exercise, muscle-relaxation techniques or meditation, a cup of tea, or some quiet music.

Early "Conversations"

In those rare moments when she is alert—as you bend over her during a diaper change, when you're lifting her out of the stroller, or especially after a feeding or nap—you can begin the process of "introducing" yourself to her. Don't worry about saying or doing "the right thing"; just do what comes naturally. Your smile, some whispered sweet nothings, or a playful recap of your day ("Remember how we woke up at *five?* And Mommy put on her robe, and *you* had breakfast, and then *Mommy* had breakfast," and so on) are all you need to enjoy a sense of communion with the tiny, precious person who has so recently come into your life.

Questions Parents Ask . . .

Q. My baby is six weeks old, but I still can't tell what she wants when she cries. Sometimes she goes on crying for an hour at a time, and I can't do anything to comfort her. I've read in several baby-care books that babies only cry when they need something, and that parents can recognize what each cry means. Help!

THE PORTABLE BABY

Babies are born voyeurs. Naturally, you don't need to set up an elaborate "program" of moving baby from one place to another as though she were on a package tour. But as you do your daily chores and errands—making beds, watering plants, visiting the dry cleaner—bring her along. And rather than letting her languish in the crib for hours on end, transfer her occasionally from carriage to infant seat to front carrier, and sometimes to a blanket on the floor. Hang a rattle on the handle or hood, where she can see it (about twelve inches from her face).

A. Some babies under three months do seem to cry a great deal for no apparent reason, but this usually tapers off as they get used to life outside the womb. In the meantime, keep in mind that although researchers using highly sophisticated technological aids—not just the human ear—can identify various kinds of cries, not all babies have cries that are easy to tell apart. At home, it takes time for a parent or caregiver to learn to distinguish one cry from another. And many parents *never* feel they can recognize an "I'm hungry" cry or an "I'm bored" cry.

Q. I'm blessed with a quiet, easygoing baby. She's almost two months old and still seems to sleep most of the day. When she wakes up, she lies quietly in her crib and doesn't even cry for me to come. Should I let her play on her own or spend more time talking to her when she is awake?

A. Your baby is so young that there is no need to get too worried about stimulating her at this point. There is no need to force social contact on her when she clearly doesn't appreciate it. She will benefit, however, from some loving give-and-take while you are changing her diapers, after a feeding, and at bath time. Instead of leaving her in her crib for prolonged periods, you might put her in an infant seat and keep her with you as you go about your daily activities.

Q. My two-month-old just sits in her infant seat at dinner and stares off into space, even when we talk to her directly. I'm worried that she is not getting any language stimulation.

A. If your baby is happy to be in her infant seat, she may be one of those infants who enjoys the sound of human talk. Just because she seems to be staring off into space doesn't mean that she isn't actually listening to you. Babies do not consistently look toward a sound they hear until about three months.

THREE

✿

Two to Eight Months: "You and Me Together"

Finally, the bright-eyed, active baby you were expecting all along has emerged. At some point after your baby's two-month birthday, you will notice a marked change from his newborn self. Now, instead of slipping from awake to drowsy and back again in an apparently random way, he is alert for longer periods of time and his responses are more organized. As one mother put it, baby seems "more like a person" now. Not surprisingly, baby's increased awareness brings changes in the communication patterns between parent and child. Suddenly your hours together expand from the kinds of interactions that seem to amount to *his* crying and *your* trying to figure out why. You and your baby will find yourselves "talking"—through your words, his coos and babbles, and lots of body language on both sides—for the sheer pleasure of it. He is a little companion with a

lot to say, one who still cries to tell you he
needs something but also has other ways to
communicate. Perhaps the most exciting of all
is his newfound use of vocalization, as he begins to coo and, later, to babble. Your baby is
only beginning to be interested in the world
of objects, and won't be able to grasp them
reliably for another three months. Nor will his
developing motor skills be a "top priority"
until he begins to creep and walk. For now,
his major interest—particularly between two
and six months—is people. He loves looking
at them, smiling and getting a smile in return, and—most of all—being talked to. You'll
probably find yourself having "conversations" in which you chime in with baby's coos
to create a charming duet. "Who's Mommy's
little angel?" you ask as you're changing his
diaper. You pause for an answer, and sure
enough, baby provides one in the form of an
attentive look, joyous smile, and cycling arms
and legs. "You *are* my angel, aren't you?"
More smiles and coos. "And you're getting to
be such a *big* boy! We're going to have to start
buying bigger diapers soon! Isn't that so?"
And baby responds once more. Although he
still isn't doing any real *talking*, your baby is
discovering a whole new world as he begins
to listen to speech sounds *and* to produce
them. The delight he takes in this process is
the bedrock of his future language development.

Growing and Changing: The Context for Communication

Your Child's Developing Body

Now that your baby is alert for longer periods, he will be more interested in looking at the world around him. During these months, he establishes regular nap times—usually one in the morning and another after lunch. This gives *you* an opportunity to rest up for his waking moments, when he'll be eager for plenty of interaction.

Interestingly enough, this is a time when several different aspects of your baby's motor development seem to "conspire" to foster his social development, and with it, his skill as a communicator. First of all, at this age baby learns to sit, first with support and then on his own. Now he can face you for a "chat," almost like a dinner partner in a restaurant! Some will sit up as early as five months, although others will not sit without support until nearly eight months.

Second, because he has not yet learned to creep or walk, baby—unlike his on-the-go toddler sibling—is perfectly happy to sit still for long periods. (You might call him a "captive audience," except that he's delighted to be right where he is.) Most babies do not creep until eight months or later, and at that time they become tireless explorers, fascinated by the feel, tastes, and sounds of the world. For now, though, he depends on you for stimulation—not in the form of Mozart recordings or flash cards, but the sight of your face and the sound of your voice.

Finally, baby is only learning to grasp objects, and will not be skillful at handling and playing with them for several months. At two months he is just beginning to notice his hands, but it is as though they were not attached to him; he cannot consciously control their movements. If given an object to touch, he will explore it with his fingers alone, not with eyes and hands coordinated, or acting together. By three months he does make the connection between hand and eye, and his hands become a favorite "toy" as he watches them move and begins swiping at objects. But it is not until five or six months of age that most babies can actually reach and grasp, and not until six or seven months that they can transfer objects from one hand to the other. In these months before the baby acquires this dexterity, people are his only real playthings. And you—the amazing walking, talking, smiling parent—are the best toy of all!

Making Sense of the World

One of the most exciting aspects of a child's cognitive development during this period is the way he begins to develop the concept of *contingency,* the idea of "If I do this, that will happen." If he swipes at a crib gym, the smiling figures begin to dance. If he kicks the sides of his crib, his blanket moves. He comes to learn not only that he can *cause* an event, but also that he can *prolong* its duration. How does this relate to communication? In a nutshell, baby now understands that when he cries or makes a noise, you respond. Not surprisingly, at about five months he begins to use his cry intentionally, as a way of summoning you. Most of the time he's been telling you he's hungry, or stuck in an uncomfortable position, or wet. But sometimes he just wants company, and he's learned that this is a surefire way to get it! Cries aren't the only way babies learn to "call" adults. One baby of five months quickly discovered that his cough—which had a slightly strangled edge to it—was a guaranteed way to bring his mother over in a matter of seconds, and cough he did! Then there was the six-month-old who developed a fake sneeze to get the same kind of result.

Contrary to common lore about "spoiling" babies, research shows that babies who are promptly responded to during these early months are less likely to turn out to be fussy, cranky, demanding children. For this reason, during these early months it is much better for a parent or caregiver to err on the side of humoring the baby who wants company. The baby has learned that by his own vocalizing, he can affect other people. And this is, after all, one of the primary reasons we use language at any age. Without a doubt, you do need to find a reasonable balance between helping empower your child to realize that he can influence others, and making it clear that you have your own legitimate needs. In due time he will have to learn to temper his own needs and desires with some respect for the autonomy of others. But all in all, baby's attempts at vocally reaching out are a wonderful development.

A Social Creature

Chances are your baby has just started smiling. You'll notice him doing a lot of that over the next few months. The period from about two to six months is one of intense sociability, a time when baby and caregivers spend much of their time in the give-and-take of communication. Dr. Daniel Stern of the Cornell University Medical Center, who has done some of the most extensive studies of mother-infant interactions, calls this the *most exclusively social* period of life. It is also the time when baby begins to distinguish between those people who are "special" to him—parents, siblings, grandparents, regular caregivers—and those who are not. In fact, by the time the baby is eight months old he will protest when you or a familiar caregiver tries to leave him with someone he does not know well. Instead of being the gregarious fellow he was only a few weeks earlier, flashing a smile at every comer, now the baby soberly examines new faces from the safety of his mother's arms. Some babies may only tone down their customary exuberance to an expression of cautious interest, but others become very fearful and cling to Mother as if for dear life. Although this behavior may prove awkward at times—say, when Great-Aunt Sue interprets it as a personal rejection—keep in mind that it is a sign of your baby's healthy bond with you. Psychiatrist Stanley Greenspan, coauthor of *First Feelings* (1985), has discovered that although infants under five months or so are content to be cared for by anyone who will meet their needs, they do gaze at their parents in a special way that Greenspan calls an "enraptured" look and is reserved strictly for Mom and Dad. By the end of this period, your baby will make it clear (with beaming smile, eye contact, and hugs) that he is very attached to you. As his language skills develop, he will also reserve many of his "sweet nothings," from coos to babbles, for those he is growing to love.

Language Learning Now

Along with your baby's new awareness of the world comes an explosion of interest in two basic elements of communication: *sounds* (both listening to them and producing them) and *social interaction.* All sorts of sounds— anything from a car horn to a French horn— will draw his attention, far more so than they did during his first weeks of life. But like his newborn self, he remains most fascinated by the sound of human voices. One three-month-old boy became fussy every evening at dinnertime, until his mother began simply bringing him into the dining room in his infant seat. The baby, she discovered, happily entertained himself by looking from one person to another during dinner conversation. And why should this be surprising? Now that the baby has learned to look for the sources of sounds, he's bound to be delighted with the combined opportunity to enjoy his two favorite stimuli, human faces and human voices.

At about two months all babies begin to make more sounds that are definite and intentional. Indeed, infant vocalization is universal—even among deaf babies, who go through the early stages of babbling in much the same way as hearing babies. This clearly indicates that these developmental stages are a function of the nervous system's maturity rather than environmental control. The *kinds* of sounds your baby makes undergo a change after two months, as well. Instead of producing the newborn's barnyard snorts and snuffles, the baby gains some control over his mouth and tongue muscles, which means he can also begin to control the sounds he makes. Now, when he's feeling happy and alert, he begins to produce the sounds known as cooing. Like most parents, you probably find these soft, warm sounds irresistible and end up "chiming in" with your own adult versions of them ("oooh," "aaah"). By about three months the baby will be spending long periods in vocal play on his own, or with a partner, just cooing away happily! As he gets older and has more practice, he will coo for longer and longer periods. Another delightful sound that you'll begin to hear sometime between two and four months is the laugh or chuckle. For sheer joy, it's hard to think of anything to match it—except the baby's smile!

Once the baby has become an "expert" cooer—which means he has quite a bit of control over his mouth and tongue—he begins to produce another type of vocalization: babbling. Instead of the soft, vowellike sounds of cooing, the baby now says things that sound very much like speech. At four or five months, he may occasionally say "nnn" or "mmm," although he is not likely to combine vowel and consonant sounds (to produce, say, "ma" or "pa"). There is *no* evidence that babies follow any sort of predictable pattern of sound acquisition—whether or not Johnny is the first on the block to say "ba" tells very little about his stage of language development—but some researchers do believe that between the ages of four and seven months baby babbling seems to change in one important way. At this stage, instead of producing sounds more or less at random, babies tend to focus more on those of the particular language spoken in their home environment. Some students of baby babble have even been able to distinguish between that of infants living in French, Arabic, and Chinese homes! Before this age, however, not even trained phoneticians can pick up differences.

Before long the baby will begin to produce his first syllablclike sounds, such as *pa, da,*or *ma.* Although we'd all like to believe that the seven-month-old who says "ma" is calling his beloved mother, the fact is that at this stage such sounds are without meaning to him. For now, he is just busy producing sounds, progressing sometime between six and ten months to what is technically known as "canonical babbling," or repetitions of the same

---

MOTHER GOOSE

It's not too early to start reciting Mother Goose rhymes and other poems to your baby. Even though he won't understand a word, you will be surprised at how attentively he listens. Babies love the rhythms and rhymes. Finger-plays such as "This Little Piggy" and "Pat-a-Cake" are also fun, and after a while you will notice him antic- ipating favorite parts (". . . and *this* little piggy cried, 'Wee, wee, wee' all the way home!"). These are time-honored ways to help him not only learn about the sounds of language, but also enjoy taking part in "conversation."

---

syllable: "dadadada," "mamamama," and "yayaya," to name a few classic examples. Soon after this stage you're likely to begin hearing a few real words, usually Dada, Mama, ba-ba (for "bottle") and—not for the last time!—the word *no*.

But the journey into language is by no means summed up by your baby's growing ability to produce regular sounds, any more than it will be later on by his knowing how to produce meaningful words or grammatically correct sentences. In addition to learning to follow linguistic patterns, every child must learn to use speech in ways that are *socially* appropriate—eventually learning to say "Please" instead of "I want," for example. Surprising though it may seem, some of the rudiments of these rules are implicitly taught in everyday parent-infant interaction even during this early period. Through your babble conversations, baby encounters certain basic conventions: for example, between three and four months, baby learns his first sociolinguistic rule—speak when spoken to. Now, when you speak to him, he responds to you with "talk" of his own. (Of course, as any parent of a four-year-old knows, these "lessons" need some supplementing later on!) Slowly, he also learns that speakers in a conversation must take turns. Notice how he begins to listen attentively (and quietly) when you speak, and then starts his "reply" only when you have finished.

What makes these interactions so compelling for baby now is that mothers, fathers, grandparents, and other loving adults take delight in providing him with just the kind of social input he loves best. Looking at the baby, and waiting for him to make eye contact, we talk to him in a special, singsong way that experts term "motherese": we pitch our voices higher, simplify our sentence structure, lengthen the vowels in our words ("soooooo big!"), and speak much more slowly than usual. Like an actor in a melodrama, we go from a stage whisper to exaggerated exclamations, and our facial expressions are hammy, to put it mildly. We also "hook" baby into interactions by imitating him, especially

---

SOUNDS

Crumpling up wrapping paper, ripping up old magazines, or shaking plastic measuring spoons are always fun for baby, and they offer early "lessons" in the associations between sounds and events. When you hear spoons clicking together, you may find yourself exclaiming: "Clickity-click, clickity-click. Where did that come from?" Through your spontaneous reactions, you are helping your baby learn to link certain sounds with the actions that cause them: "When I shake this, it makes a noise." Likewise, old-fashioned baby games like "I'm gonna get you!" and "Where's the baby?" also help an infant associate sounds (or words) and events. Before you know it, all you need to do is say, "I'm gonna get you!" and your baby will be crawling down the hall and around the corner at top speed.

---

his funny facial expressions and interesting sounds. Perhaps most remarkable is the way we hold our infants close and tenderly in our arms, gazing long and deep into their eyes— body language that clearly says "I love you" at any age. All this amounts to the perfect "display" for baby, who, as you may recall, is preadapted to favor high-pitched voices and facial movement.

While the infant is still in the cooing stage, the intensity of baby's fascination with loving adults is what makes it possible for us to create what one researcher calls a "communication frame," a structure that helps incorporate his new social behaviors (eye contact, smiling, babbling, and so on) into a conversation of sorts. As Chicago psychologist Dr. Kenneth Kaye explains it in his book *The Mental and Social Life of Babies*, parents help a baby grow into a social human being by *treating* him like a person long before he can *behave* like a person. Have you ever noticed how adults tend to "put words in baby's mouth" by attributing all sorts of preferences and ideas to infants? Grandma may be baby-sitting, for example, and discover that baby is unwilling to accept a bottle of formula. "Sammy just doesn't like my cooking!" says Grandma, turning to the allegedly finicky gourmand. *"Do* you? No! Sammy likes Mom's better!" Through these everyday "exchanges" the baby gradually learns that such a conversation is a give-and-take, long before he is able to actively participate. How nice to think that such "lessons" come naturally to most parents and infants.

Everyday Language Learning: How to Help

Far from being a "skill" learned in formal isolation, language is an inextricable part of our human heritage. Because we are social beings, communication with others is central to the way we humans live. For this reason, your baby's language development at this point depends largely on the natural physiological processes that help draw him into human social life. Since, as we have seen, parents quite naturally tend to provide the kind of feedback a baby is most suited to receive, you need no step-by-step formulas or specially designed videotapes to help your baby learn to speak. You can rest assured that the pleasure you take in getting to know your baby and sharing his company will bear fruit in the quality of your interactions. Baby will be delighted with you just as you are delighted with him. In the course of a day, there are endless opportunities for conversation in the most mundane moments—as you're taking the clothes out of the dryer ("Do you see the big hole in this sock?"), paying bills ("See this envelope? These people want us to pay them so much money!"), or unpacking your briefcase ("Look at these pretty folders in all different colors!"). Sometimes the events and

---

BALLOONS

A baby who cannot yet move from one place to another is delighted to have movement brought to him. A colorful, bobbing balloon usually captures his attention. If you have a helium balloon left over from a friend's birthday party or a fair, try tying it to baby's wrist or ankle. (Mylar is safer than rubber.) After a while, he'll notice that the balloon moves around as he moves his arm or ankle. Talk to him about what he is doing and seeing, especially after he is five or six months old.

---

activities that seem least worth talking about are the very ones that fascinate baby.

In fact, one problem many caregivers encounter is that baby, having so recently developed into a small social butterfly, now demands so much attention that he is wearing them out. He may be a wakeful baby who hardly ever naps, or one who simply cannot bear to do anything but his very favorite activity—you know, playing with Mom and Dad! Although we'd be the last to recommend you deprive the baby of adult company, do keep in mind that he can also benefit from *some* time on his own during these months. Even a three-month-old will enjoy batting at some interesting objects hung overhead—stuffed toys and rattles, small noisemakers and wooden spoons. Instead of leaving him in the solitary

confinement of his crib, set him up in a
stroller or infant seat near you, in the kitchen
or living room where you can do your chores
and chat at the same time. One mother attached a plastic hook under the edge of the
kitchen table and dangled from it a changing
assortment of trinkets on an elastic cord, then
lay her baby underneath on a blanket while
she and her husband sat down to work on the
month's bills. Once baby can sit (on his own
or propped up by cushions), you can provide
him with plenty of interesting objects to explore. (Be careful, of course, not to give him
anything he could swallow or hurt himself
with.) By the time baby can sit up, he has also
learned to grasp and his attention will shift
toward object play, making him less exclusively social and taking some of the pressure
off Mom and Dad.

Ironically, the danger for parents who are
especially eager to foster language development is that in our enthusiasm we can unwit-
tingly sabotage nature's plan. Perhaps you've
heard some timeworn advice about language
learning: "If you want a baby to talk, you have
to talk to him a lot." With the six-month-old
baby, this maxim can be an invitation to dis-
aster. You can chatter away *at* him and not,
in fact, help him very much at a time when
your baby is meant to be establishing a pattern for normal human interaction. Furthermore, in her research Paula Menyuk of Boston

University has found that parents' nonstop
talking is *not* helpful to infant language development. The babies Menyuk studied developed better language skills when their
mothers paused between sentences as though
expecting a reply. Rather than delivering a
forced lecture on the beauty of a spring morning—"The sky is blue, the birds are chirping,
the grass is green, the air is warm, you can
wear your sailor hat"—it is far more effective
for a parent or caregiver to ask a simple question and wait for an answer: "Did Danny hear
that birdie chirping outside?" Then pause and
wait for the baby's answer, which might be
anything from a smile to a gurgle. (If the use
of the child's proper name, rather than the
pronoun *you*, strikes you as strange, keep in
mind that it's much less confusing to a young
child. When you stop to think about it, the
meanings of pronouns such as *I* and *you* are
not easy to pin down, since they continually
change depending on who is talking!) At bath
time, or while he "helps" you fix dinner, or
on the way to the store, look for opportunities
for dialogue about what is going on. He will
be delighted to learn the names of unfamiliar
objects and places (from a mailbox to a bar-
bershop), and to discuss the comings and
goings of trains, cars, even the sun and moon.

The second problem with "talking a lot" is
that to a baby of this age certain kinds of talking will sound like nothing more than a bar-

rage of words. We're referring not to the obvious—say, abstract discourses on your wine preferences—but even to chatting with your child about what he did yesterday. During this period and for many months to come he will be most responsive to language tied in with the here and now. Cognitively speaking, he does not engage in the kind of abstract thinking done by adults and older children. What he can understand are those things he is seeing, touching, tasting, or smelling. Fortunately, this is exactly the kind of conversation that arises naturally out of the nitty-gritty of everyday life with a baby. "Would you like some *juice?*" you ask as you offer your eight-month-old his cup. Or "No!" as you pull your new creeper away from an electrical outlet. In dozens of repetitions of this sort over many days and weeks, your baby will begin to realize that words are associated with particular things.

There's another problem about making up your mind to "talk a lot," and in many ways it's the most serious one of all. Simply put, your baby just may not like it. Just as adults run the gamut from the "life of the party" to the "strong, silent type," even at this typically sociable age there are some babies who prefer time alone. This is likely to be a reflection of temperament. If a baby is relatively unenthusiastic about early communication games, a parent or caregiver may worry that

---

MOTION

Bouncing baby on your knee as you listen to music, or actually dancing around the room with him: these are wonderful ways you can offer baby the opportunity to enjoy movement and sound, and to experience the pleasure of words set to music. The music can be anything from a Raffi or Wee Sing tape to your rendition of a favorite sixties' song (say, a slightly off-key "She Loves You").

---

he will not have enough experience with language to learn to talk. But in the course of the day, you may be surprised at how much interaction really occurs between you. In the course of day-to-day caregiving even the quiet baby usually gives parents or sitter plenty of opportunities for socializing, and the presence of these moments provides clear evidence that your baby is developing normally. There are those times when he catches your eye while you're changing his diaper, for example, or looks up with an inquiring expression during a feeding. Sometimes you can catch his attention by imitating the sounds he makes, which may pique his interest enough to bring his gaze to you.

Let the baby tell you he is ready for play by looking at you expectantly. Those are the moments to do silly imitations: when he smacks his lips, you smack yours. If he says "aaah," you can join in. He will not be ready to imitate *your* sounds until around the age of eight months, but at this stage your aping him will give him great delight—not to mention the opportunity to mimic *you* right back with an "aaah!" of his own! (At this stage babies *can* imitate actions and sounds that are already in their repertoires, but it is not until after eight months or so that they can imitate ones that are *new* to them.) On the other hand, if your baby seems to be avoiding eye contact, there's no point pushing it; he'll only be unhappy and continue to avert his gaze. And always stop the "conversation" when you see that baby— who is averting his eyes, turning his head away, or beginning to arch his back—has had enough.

It's not always easy to understand baby's cues, particularly if his temperamental "style" is very different from your own. In fact, according to the pioneering researchers on temperament Stella Chess and Alexander Thomas, "goodness of fit," or the parents' sensitivity to the child's personality style, is actually more important to a child's development than the nature of his particular temperament. Even the most flamboyant child will thrive as long as his parents' demands and expectations are compatible with his abilities and strong personality. If, on the other hand, your baby is easygoing but shy and *you* are highly gregarious, you may find it difficult to avoid intruding on his need for nonsocial time. In your eagerness to "connect" you may ignore his cues that he has had enough. You may pursue him to the point that his only option is to "fuss out" or fall asleep. It's a vicious cycle: he retreats and you pursue, causing him to retreat still further until you feel thoroughly rejected. Sometimes you may even end up drawing away from him in your disappointment and frustration. Obviously, if this pattern becomes an ongoing one, it does little to enhance your relationship and is likely, in fact, to interfere with it. As for language learning, Katherine Nelson of the City University of New York has found that when parents cannot accept their children's early communication styles, the children make *slower language progress* than those whose parents are accepting of their individual approach to and style of communication.

When we find it difficult to reconcile ourselves to our child's peculiar social style, we are presented with one of many opportunities in our lives as parents to ponder some of the fundamental questions about the nature of our relationship with our child. We discussed some in Chapter One—questions that affect not only language but every other aspect of our child's development. When we talk or play with him, are we genuinely willing to appreciate him as another person, or do we see him as an object of sorts, an extension of ourselves

who is expected to provide us with ego grati-
fication? Even though your baby is only beginning to get the faintest glimmer that he is
a separate person from you, as a parent *you*
can help start your relationship on the right
foot by respecting his individuality. Expecting our child to communicate *our* way is a
sign that we are not acknowledging him as a
separate person. One mother we know found
it difficult to know how to approach her
daughter, a colicky newborn who grew into a
not-very-cuddly baby. "I'm very affectionate,
and she always seemed to hate hugging," said
the mother. It was not until her child was a
toddler that this mother learned to accept the
fact that her baby's behavior was a reflection
of temperament and physical sensitivity
rather than a personal rejection, and to allow
the baby to communicate in her own way.
"Now that she's talking I'm enjoying the fact
that she has a mind of her own," she says
now. "Things would have been a lot easier if
I'd learned not to try to force *my* style on
her."

Another side effect of seeing our child as an
extension of ourselves is that it is all too
tempting to push him into performing skills
for which he is not yet ready, or to become
alarmed when he is not saying "dada" as
early as the "clever" baby down the block.
After all, isn't each new skill our baby learns
a source of pride and a reflection of our own

parenting ability? Remember, though, that much of what babies do in the early months is primarily dictated by nervous-system maturation. Some babies will be smiling at the mail carrier and grocery clerk by two months, while others only begin to offer tentative smiles to Mom and Dad at three months. Likewise, many perfectly normal babies begin to coo, laugh, and babble at different times during this period. A baby who develops these behaviors slightly later than his peers (assuming he is within the normal range) is at no disadvantage, because there is *no* evidence to show that a slow rate of maturation correlates with poor language skills at later ages. The old expression "late bloomer" is an apt one to remember. Is the bloom any less lovely because it comes in August rather than in June? The developments of these months offer an important message for the parent who is willing to listen: as your baby grows, you are going to find that when you are willing to relax, let him be himself, and let nature take its course, you are in for some lovely surprises from him. A communication style all his own is beginning to unfold.

Questions Parents Ask . . .

Q. My baby is six months old. He used to love our little "conversations" and talk to me with wonderful chuckles and giggles. Now he seems to prefer to spend long periods sitting on the floor playing by himself. Am I doing something wrong?

A. Your baby is showing signs of growth. A few months ago you were his best entertainment, because he could do so little on his own. Now he can sit up and probably use his hands well, and he's exploring the exciting new world of objects. You can encourage him by providing plenty of safe things of different colors, textures, and weights—rattles, jars, toy musical instruments, and the like. Talk to him about the things he is exploring, but also allow him some time to do his exploring without interruption.

Q. My baby seems to babble more in the morning than in the evening. Is there any reason for this?

A. One possible reason is that he enjoys "talking" more when he's feeling fresh and rested. For a baby, babbling requires a certain amount of energy; it's no small effort to organize and produce all those different sounds!

Q. I'm a fairly quiet person. Should I force myself to talk to my baby more than I normally would, if I want to help his language development?

A. When it comes to talking, quantity is less important than quality. Talking *with* a baby about the things he is interested in, and leaving "spaces" for his responses, is far more meaningful than talking *at* him incessantly. As your baby's ability to communicate his interests increases, you are likely to find yourself naturally conversing with him—and thoroughly enjoying it, rather than forcing yourself.

Q. My child's caregiver is always talking loudly to my infant—as if this will make him understand. Should I stop this? Is it going to be bad for my baby, who sometimes just watches her, and other times looks away or even cries?

A. Assuming she is not hard of hearing, your child's caregiver may be speaking loudly because she realizes she is not getting through to the baby (just as many of us do when attempting to make ourselves understood in a foreign language). If your baby is looking away and crying, he's clearly uncomfortable with the loud tone. While the baby may adapt to this, he *may* become overstimulated and unhappy. In observing the caregiver, you may notice that she is not waiting

for signs that the baby is really ready for social interaction; why not point out that the
baby is not always ready to talk and is more
receptive when alert and making eye contact. If you also find that the caregiver tends
to talk abstractly (about events of last week
rather than objects in the here and now),
share your discoveries of some of baby's hot
topics of conversation—his hands, his toes,
his food, and his favorite rattle, for example.
With improved communication, the loud
talking is likely to disappear.

FOUR

Eight to Sixteen Months: At the Threshold

One evening several years back I received a distressed phone call from Sara, a first-time mother who had been attending one of my parents' support groups. Earlier that day she had brought her son, Mark, to the pediatrician, whose alarming diagnosis confirmed her worst fears. At the time Mark, an engaging fourteen-month-old who loved to be read to and was already fascinated by trucks, had yet to say a single word. Declaring that by this stage a child should be able at least to say "Mama" or "Dada," the pediatrician pronounced him "language-delayed."

"Is there really something wrong with him?" Sara asked me anxiously. "Or am *I* doing something wrong as a parent?" She told me she had tried everything she could think of to encourage him. From the time she dressed him in the morning (". . . and now we're putting on your *shirt"*) to his bedtime story ("Where's the bunny? Can you pat him?") she offered him every opportunity to be exposed to language. She was starting to feel embarrassed around the other mothers in Mark's play group, she said, because they were constantly comparing notes on *their* babies' new words. And several people had even criticized her for "making things too easy for Mark," advising her not to allow him any treats unless he asked for them in words!

I had a hunch there was a great deal more to Mark's language development than his spoken vocabulary seemed to indicate. "How do you communicate with each other?" I asked Sara. And sure enough, Mark could *understand* quite a few words, and he could make his needs known in various ways. For example, he would hold up his arms to her when he wanted to be picked up. If he wanted his bottle, he would find it and hold it up to her, or point to it. In fact, he used pointing to indicate a lot of his wants, along with an insistent "eh-eh-eh" which his mother called "chimp talk."

"Mark never speaks at all?" I asked.

"Well, he spends most of the day jabbering in something that sounds like a foreign language," she replied in a dejected tone.

After pressing her further on his communication skills, I realized my hunch had been right. There was nothing wrong at all with Mark's language development. What *was* a problem was his mother's lack of information about the nature of early language learning, combined with the fact that her misconceptions had been backed up by so many of her friends—not to mention her child's pediatrician. Mark—like his play group peers—was a perfectly normal toddler at the "threshold" of true language. In order to appreciate how much progress he was making, the adults in his life needed to learn how to "read" his overall communication behavior rather than simply tallying up a word count. As we saw in Chapter One, the world of language is a very wide one, and each child enters it along a slightly different path. For this reason the "threshold" period is both an exciting and a trying one for parents. It is a time when we need to remind ourselves that a child's development cannot be summarized by an abstract timetable or milestone chart. The acquisition of language, like everything else learned during this period of astonishing growth, is far more complex than that. Babies at this stage are beginning to absorb much more sophisticated linguistic concepts: that certain sounds can be associated with certain objects or actions, and that they can use vocalization (not just words, but other vocal sounds as well) and gesture as tools with which to communicate their wants. First words are the proverbial tip of the iceberg. When we understand the fact that our baby is dealing with lan-

guage on so many different levels during this
period, it becomes easier to learn how to parent our own real, live baby—not the dream
child we may have imagined before her arrival, nor the mythical one who displays every
new skill "on schedule," but the precious little person who is learning so very much in so
short a time, and in ways that are all her own.

Growing and Changing: The Context for Communication

Your Child's Developing Body

Once your baby has learned to sit up by herself, in a few months she will probably be
learning to creep or crawl, and then to walk.
Like every aspect of your child's development, these are skills she will approach with
a style and schedule that are highly individual. Although most babies choose the tradi-
tional up-on-all-fours posture for crawling,
others prefer the "crab walk," scooting
around on their bottoms and pushing or pulling themselves along with one leg. They may
begin crawling anytime between six and ten
months—and then again, some perfectly normal infants never crawl at all! Likewise, most

babies will take their first steps unaided between twelve and fourteen months, but there are perfectly normal children who do not begin to walk until sixteen months.

In short, each baby has her own "priorities." The early creeper, for example, may be so elated to discover all the interesting things she can now get her hands on—from the VCR's control panel to the telephone book whose pages are so lovely to rip—that language learning "takes a back seat" to exploration for a while. Rest assured that this is a temporary phenomenon, and there's no need to be alarmed that she's stopped learning to communicate! On the other hand, you may have an "armchair executive" who uses vocalization and gesture to charm you into bringing her the objects of her desire. Instead of worrying that she's not growing into a high-speed creeper like the baby down the block, why not instead enjoy the fact that your infant is developing her communication skills?

Whatever your baby's locomotive preferences, you will notice that by eight months she has become considerably more adept with her hands. Now, instead of pawing at objects and surfaces with her whole hand, she has very good control over her fingers and thumb. Using this new "pincer grasp" is one of her favorite pastimes, and she may be perfectly happy to spend long periods picking bits of cracker crumbs or lint out of the carpet. Handling objects of different shapes, sizes, textures, and colors will encourage her "hands-on experiments" with the world of objects, which will be the basis for her talk later on. Hearing the names of objects she's handling, and the words to describe them ("Look at this block. Can you feel how hard it is? Not soft, like the pillow.") will help her develop language. And discovering that she can pick up an object, shake it, perhaps cause it to make a noise, will reinforce her sense of self as someone who can affect her environment.

Making Sense of the World

The period from eight to twelve months is a ground-breaking one because it heralds what developmentalists believe is an important advance in baby's intellectual growth: goal-directed behavior. Now, instead of simply noticing that things happen, the baby begins to realize that she can *make* them happen—and to try and figure out how. She has become a thinking, problem-solving being. According to the pioneering studies by Jean Piaget, the twentieth-century Swiss philosopher and psychologist whose observations of cognitive development in babies laid the foundation for our understanding of their mental growth, this is a time when the baby not only begins to set goals—such as "getting that cracker on the floor behind the newspaper''—but also discovers various means to achieve them. In order to get her chubby fingers around that cracker, she will now either maneuver herself around the newspaper or simply move the pages aside.

Your baby's burgeoning interest in objects extends to slapping, banging, waving, mouthing, and throwing virtually anything she can get hold of. Not only is she having a wonderful time, but she is also learning about their characteristics—how each object tastes and feels in her mouth, how far it can be tossed, how heavy or light it is, whether it is rough or smooth. As you see her fingering or mouthing an object, you'll probably find yourself offering impromptu "language lessons" by providing baby with the words for these concepts: "Is that lemon bitter?" "Isn't teddy soft?" "Do the wheels on that truck turn?"

At this stage, your baby may also begin to include you in her problem-solving "experiments." If you show her something particularly interesting—say, a toy xylophone that chimes when you hammer it—she may draw the conclusion that by pushing on your hand, she can get you to make music! And she will probably enjoy that favorite game of the highchair set, I Drop the Toy and You Pick It Up. Your ten-month-old is not only fascinated by the different effects she can produce with each toss of the toy—how far she can make it land,

and what sound it makes—but also by the opportunity to turn *you* into a handy means to achieve her ends. Although you may feel manipulated and even frustrated at times, try to remember that she is not trying to "drive you crazy" but is merely exercising her new mental abilities.

A Social Creature

In the last chapter we discussed your baby's new attachment to you and other regular caregivers. Now her developing powers allow her to cement that attachment in myriad ways. She begins to appreciate humor, especially when Dad or another grown-up does something silly, such as wearing a diaper on his head or trying to suck on her upturned bottle. And she is becoming what researchers refer to as a "social presence," which may strike many parents as quite an understatement in light of her attempts to follow you anywhere you try to go—including the bathroom! You will probably discover that your baby's goal-directed behavior also naturally extends to her ability to keep track of you. When you pick up your car keys, for example, she instantly deduces that you're going out and clings desperately to your leg. Or the sitter arrives at the door and she begins to whimper. At this time she is likely to be shy or even frightened of people she does not recognize, depending on her temperament. *Your* reaction will also affect your baby's response. Researchers at the University of Colorado have discovered that babies engage in "social referencing," a term used to describe the way babies of this age learn to interpret their parents' nonverbal cues about strangers. In one 1983 study, when mothers greeted a stranger entering a room in a friendly way, the babies looked to Mom and, seeing her positive reaction, displayed interest in the new arrival. When mothers seemed cautious, however, their babies became fearful.

You might be surprised to know not only how adept your baby is at reading your signals, but how eager she is to do so. In a famous series of experiments at the University of Colorado, twelve-month-old babies were placed on a Plexiglass tabletop divided into two sections: one lined with a checkerboard pattern that gave it the appearance of a solid floor, and the other with the checkerboard pattern lowered twelve inches below the Plexiglass to create a "visual cliff." In one experiment, mothers were asked to coax their babies to the edge of this "cliff." Ordinarily, when a baby of this age is creeping across the checkerboard section, she will stop at the edge of the "cliff" and refuse to cross. When one group of mothers stopped coaxing and acted alarmed as their babies neared the edge, their babies followed the usual pattern and stayed put on the checkerboard section. But when another group of mothers was instructed to coax their babies "across the cliff," most of the infants actually were willing to continue over the "edge," as long as their mothers seemed relaxed and confident. They trusted their mothers' signals more than their own perception!

Language Learning Now

Now is a time when many parents await with mounting anticipation their baby's very first word. Sometime during this threshold period, many children—though by no means all of them—will make their first attempts to pronounce full-fledged "real" words, as opposed to babbling. Try to keep in mind that your becoming anxious about the timing of that first "grown-up" word does absolutely nothing to enhance your child's language development, not to mention the quality of your relationship. Rest assured that before long you'll find it hard to remember the day when your child *wasn't* talking. One mother who was getting worried because her twelve-month-old had yet to say "Mommy" shared her concern with an older neighbor. "Don't worry," the neighbor advised good-naturedly.

"Before you know it he'll be calling you so often it'll drive you nuts!"

Besides, to focus on the first word as the sole evidence of your child's communication growth is to ignore many other exciting signs of her language development. Have you noticed the way her babbling has been changing to include sounds that are distinctly word-like? Isn't it amazing the way she seems to understand at least something of what you tell her? Has she begun to communicate not only by crying, but by actively signaling to the nearest adult that she needs help? There is still a long road ahead before your child can really use language in an adult sense, but the child in this threshold period has taken command of a very important idea: that vocalization and gesture (like creeping and grasping) are tools she can use to accomplish many of her goals.

What is perhaps most exciting about this period is that it heralds what linguists call *intentional communication,* or baby's deliberate attempts to tell you something. She is beginning to realize that she can use sounds to tell you things—that she's excited, or hungry, or unhappy. She lets out an angry "eeeh," for example, when you refuse her a sip of your Scotch. She succeeds in getting your attention and keeping it, perhaps by holding out her arms and squealing "aaah!" the minute you return home from work. She can make a request, in the way she crawls to the kitchen counter and says "eh-eh" as she points to a bowl of bananas. And she can make it abundantly clear that you—and no one else—are the adult she has chosen for the privilege of picking up the baby doll she has thrown from the high-chair.

Now she uses eye contact not only as a signal that she is ready for social play, but in order to let us know what she wants. At six or seven months, she would "tell" you she was hungry by looking at her bottle and fussing. Now, however, at eight or nine months, she still fusses, she still looks at the bottle, but she also looks *from bottle to you*—a virtually unmistakable signal that she not only wants the bottle, but wants *you* to give it to her!

In a related development, you may notice that your baby has learned to "escalate her demands." Now, if one form of communication doesn't seem to be working, she tries something else—reaching for the bottle and bouncing, for instance! Fortunately, she is also beginning to learn to read her caregivers' goals and intentions. If you do decide to get up and head for the bottle in the refrigerator, she is likely to stop fussing because she realizes her request is about to be granted.

Let's take a closer look at several particularly fascinating areas of communication growth that contribute to your baby's newfound expressiveness. For one thing, she is beginning to make great strides in her *comprehension* of language. Perhaps you've noticed that she usually turns toward you now when you say her name. Or she may have developed an uncanny ability to pick up words that are important in her life, even in the middle of an adult conversation. One mother we know was talking with her husband on the telephone one afternoon while her ten-month-old daughter scooted around the house in a walker, and in the course of their chat she suggested he pick up a bottle of wine for dinner. Before she knew it, the baby had dashed off to the living room and wheeled herself back to the kitchen with—you guessed it!—her own plastic bottle in hand and an eager smile on her face!

Most children begin to understand some individual words during the period from eight to ten months, and by thirteen months their "comprehension vocabulary" may range from fifteen or so to nearly one hundred words, although (as in all language development) there are great differences from one baby to another even among normal children. Once the baby has begun to get the idea that certain sounds are associated with certain objects or events in her world, her comprehension vocabulary grows rapidly. Soon after her first birthday you may find yourself having to resort to spelling a few key words: "Shall we go for a

W-A-L-K?" or "Maybe we should let her have
her B-O-T-T-L-E a little early tonight." Unfortunately for parents, babies learn the words
for their favorite activities and treats long before they can grasp abstract concepts such as
"not right now" or "later"!

Oddly enough, the baby's growing ability to
understand words does not automatically
lead to her *say* them. Often there is a surprisingly long time lag between the two steps.
Your child's first spoken words may be entirely different from the first words she comes
to understand. And in fact, researchers have
discovered that the children with the largest
spoken vocabularies at this age do *not* necessarily turn out to be the earliest or best talkers. In short, there is little relation between a
child's understanding of language and her
production of it during these early months
and years.

The production of words is part of a complex process that gradually emerges from
babbling. As you have probably noticed, she
is continuing to babble, but not in exactly the
same way. Instead of the canonical babbling
we discussed in Chapter Three, in which she
simply repeated a *single* vowel-consonant
combination ("mama," "baba"), the baby
now begins to string together combinations of
different vowels and consonants ("dadu,"
"papu"). She also may add sentence intonation. The result is a new kind of babbling

---

WHERE'S SPOT?

Even before your baby has said her first word,
she will be ready for a simple pointing game.
Start with body parts—hers and your own. As
you're wiping food off her chin after dinner, ask,
"Where's Lizzie's chin? Where's Lizzie's nose?
Where's Mommy's nose?" Once she's learned to
play this version of the pointing game, expand
to the dog or cat, and to pictures of people and
animals. For a tricky variation, try it in front of
a mirror; she won't realize that the baby in the
mirror is herself until she's some sixteen to
twenty months old, but will enjoy pointing to
her reflection anyway.

---

known as baby *jargon,* when the child sounds
for all the world as if she is producing sentences and even paragraphs, but all in a foreign language!

Keep in mind that babies differ greatly in
the extent to which they use jargon. There are
those who spend much of the day in long so-
liloquy, and others who hardly speak in jargon at all. Here's a rather striking illustration
of one of our fundamental points—that two
perfectly normal babies are likely to have entirely different ways of learning language and
yet both somehow develop into children who
can talk, probably more than their parents
ever dreamed possible! Dr. John Dore of the
City University of New York has broadly cat-

egorized children of this age as "intonation" babies (who love to use jargon) and "word" babies (who begin speaking in words without first using sounds that resemble adult sentence-intonation patterns). The "word" babies seem to focus on the referential aspects of language—what the individual words mean, rather than how sentences sound as a whole. To some parents, they may appear more advanced because they begin to learn "real words" before their intonation-oriented peers. On the other hand, we know one mother who fretted for several months because her baby "never talked baby talk" (that is, never produced jargon), and was then surprised and delighted to find her infant daughter "suddenly coming out with full-blown *words*—out of thin air!" As for "intonation" babies, do you remember Mark, the fourteen-month-old whose mother, Sara, called me in alarm because he was supposedly language-delayed? He was a classic example of the infant whose early experiments with language seem to focus more on its sound contours. Babies in this "intonation" group begin to speak by producing a series of nonsense sentences whose intonation mimics that of adult speakers. You might hear your infant chattering away in jargon on a toy telephone, for example, as though she's animatedly relaying a choice tidbit of gossip. Obviously, it would be simplistic to suggest that there are only *two* kinds of babies. These categories probably represent two ends on a continuum, and most babies fall somewhere between the two extremes. You may well discover that your beginning talker speaks in her own special blend of words and jargon.

During this period, many babies also begin to produce one or more *wordlike sounds* or "invented words," that they consistently use to refer to particular objects or events. Although these are not real adult words, caregivers quickly catch on to their meanings. In one of Piaget's famous observations of his own children's behavior, he noted that his daughter Jacqueline always used the sound "tch-tch" to refer to vehicles she saw passing by a certain window in their home. Not surprisingly, one of the most popular invented words among babies seems to mean "I want"; it often sounds something like "eh-eh-eh" and is often accompanied by a pointed finger or an enthusiastic body bounce.

At some point between ten and fourteen months, your baby will probably say her *first real word,* although her pronunciation is likely to vary considerably from standard English. Unlike adult words, these very early words tend to be "stuck" to particular contexts. One fourteen-month-old's first word, "goggie," referred only to one particular "doggie" sitting on one particular doorstep. For this child no other dog, and not even the same dog in another location, counted as a real "goggie." To cite one of many similar examples, the daughter of one researcher used the word *kitty* only upon throwing her stuffed cat out of the crib.

What invented words like *tch-tch* have in common with *kitty, goggie,* and other early words is that they are meaningful to baby only within a very narrow range of situations. Most language specialists believe that babies at this stage do not realize that words actually *stand for* their referents—that each word represents a concept, the way the word *cat* symbolizes a four-legged feline that purrs. Instead, the baby seems to understand each word at this stage as an inherent aspect of an individual object itself, and to view each object as unique unto itself in all the world. She is a bit like that favorite of satirists, the foreigner who visits McDonald's for the first time and assumes it is just one small restaurant where hamburgers are served in cardboard boxes. In time, of course, he learns that he has seen a particular example of a phenomenon far more widespread than he had ever imagined. Likewise, during the next few months, your baby will come to use words in increasingly broader contexts. Soon, "kitty" will be her word not only for your striped tabby, but for any cat she sees. In a few more months, her concept of *cat* may even extend to include your pet's wild cousins, such as the tiger and leopard.

But she has already come a long way in the past year. From the newborn whose instinctive cry could only tell you that she needed *something*—food? sleep? a clean diaper?—she has grown into a surprisingly effective little communicator who uses eye contact, gesture, and an assortment of vocalizations to explain herself in no uncertain terms.

Everyday Language Learning: How to Help

Researchers have observed a number of subtle yet fascinating ways parents naturally adapt their responses to accommodate their babies' development during this period. According to Dr. Daniel Stern of the Cornell University Medical Center in his book *The Interpersonal World of the Infant,* mothers continue to offer plenty of feedback to babies' displays of emotions, but there's an interesting difference in the pattern. Now, rather than merely imitating our babies' attempts at communication (smiling back when baby smiles, for example) as we did in previous months, we begin to change our strategy a bit. Now we show baby that we share the way she feels not by copying her behavior but by offering a variation on it. Have you noticed that when your baby lets out a joyous "ahhhh!" when you hand her a toy, you don't just say "ahhhh!" right back the way you used to? Instead, you probably find yourself reflecting her joy another way—by raising your arms and cheering softly, with wide-open eyes. With actions such as these we say to the baby, "I know just how you feel!" We show the baby that we are "tuned in" to her. And this is the kind of encouragement she needs to keep sharing her emotions with us, and expand her vocabulary of gestures and vocalization even further. For quite a while her ways of telling you things will remain mostly nonverbal, but rest assured that your natural ability to tune in to your baby's increasingly sophisticated communication skills is providing her with just the kind of encouragement she needs.

One sign of our sensitivity to the baby's needs is our tendency to give her as many opportunities as possible to *make connections between sounds and referents,* i.e., to link the word *cookie* with the sweet round objects in the cookie jar. As with all language help, there are plenty of opportunities to do this naturally in the course of your everyday routine. We would feel rather foolish darting around the kitchen in a frenzy of naming objects ("Refrigerator! Cookbooks! Applesauce!"), and in fact this approach would do little or nothing to help our babies learn. Nor do we appeal to

---

SHARING THE FUN

Have you noticed that your exchanges with baby at this stage seem to follow a pattern of "theme and variations"? For example, she drinks milk from a cup and lets out a satisfied sigh as she sets it down on the high-chair tray, and you ask, "Isn't that milk good?" Or she picks up a rattle and shakes it, and you respond by ringing a toy bell. Just as a satisfying adult conversation depends on the speakers' mutual understanding and willingness to exchange information or feelings, these interactions with baby are natural opportunities for you to show her you are attuned to her thoughts and to offer new ideas and modes of expression.

---

a baby of this age through abstract discourses about the violin sonata that was on the radio before her nap—or even the toothbrush she was holding in her hand a minute ago. Instead, simply offer her the words for concrete objects that seem to have caught her attention at this particular moment: "Oh, do you want that *cookie?*" or "You love playing with that *teddy bear,* don't you?" Follow your natural tendency to make it short and sweet: limit your sentences to a few words, and speak as clearly as possible. Above all, strike while the iron is hot—respond while the baby is still focused on the cookie or teddy. Research shows that if you delay even

---

ACTIONS AND WORDS

During a bath, your child is bound to be fascinated by water. Give her containers of all sizes and shapes, sponges, cloths—anything you don't mind getting wet—and let her fill, splash, pour, and squeeze. This is an opportunity to introduce words that can be easily linked with her actions: "Do you feel how *soft* the sponge is? Can you *pour* the water into the red pail? Try not to *spill* it all over the floor!"

---

by a minute, and baby's attention has shifted, the benefit of your response is lost.

Another important way parents naturally tend to encourage language learning at this stage is by continuing to treat babies as full-fledged *participants* in conversation—even when their "words" make no literal sense in adult terms. When you're looking at a picture book together, for example, and she points to a drawing of a chick, you ask her, "What's that?" "Eeech," she replies with a smile, and you smile right back: "That's right, it's a *baby chick!*" She, in turn, babbles some more and you laugh in response: "Yes, a chick!" And so the "game" continues. In the process of enjoying a wonderful private moment together, you are helping her learn by enabling her to *hear* the word and *see* its referent (the chick) while her attention is focused on it, and by imputing to her the ability to "hold up her

---

FRIENDLY FACES

Try filling a photo album with pictures of family and friends familiar to your toddler. Make it sturdy enough to hold up to her use, and let her have access to it just as you would her books. At this age, she will enjoy sitting down with you and naming the people in the photographs, just as you would point out pictures in a storybook. Later, you can add pictures of special events such as holidays and trips—Santa's visit, the tricycle Grandpa brought over on her birthday, the day she went for a ride in her uncle's new car. An album like this not only becomes her own personal "word" book but makes a lovely keepsake for her as she grows up.

---

end of the conversation." Thus, although she has not actually pronounced the word *chick* herself at this point, she is learning some very powerful concepts.

Do keep in mind, however, that appreciating her communication efforts in this way is very different from praising her for every new word and sound. She does not expect or need you to fall into the unfortunate pattern of acting like a cheerleader shouting hurrahs every time she says anything that sounds like a word. In fact, in the long run this all-too-common approach can even be harmful to your relationship as a whole. Let's say your child reaches for your car keys on the table

and says "ka." If you respond by *praising* her
("Key? Did baby say *key*? That's wonderful!
Oh, Mommy's so proud!") what you are doing
is shifting her focus away from her growing
ability to use language like a normal human
being—in this case to express a desire—and
turning her words into a performance to be
judged by you, or a series of linguistic
"hoops" through which you expect her to
jump. Now, you wouldn't consider being so
careless or cruel as to *tease* her about her ba-
byish pronunciation, right? Keep in mind,
however, that although praise and mockery
may seem very different, they are actually two
sides of the same coin. Your baby (and your
relationship) will benefit by your responding—with all your natural warmth and delight
at her words, of course—to *what* she says, not
the fact that she says it. In the example above,
this means saying something like, "Oh, would
you like to see these keys, sweetie pie?" and
handing them to her for a few minutes. In this
way, during this period and in the months and
years to come, she will get the message that
you accept and respect her as a conversation
partner and are *encouraging* her to continue
to use language as a way of expressing her
feelings and needs. She will know that you
take pleasure not only in the achievement her
growing vocabulary represents, but in the
unique individual her newfound expressiveness is revealing her to be.

KABOOM!

Building towers and knocking them down is a favorite game at this age, and don't be surprised if your child begins to imitate the "Bang!" or "Kaboom!" you exclaim as the tower hits the floor. Young children love hearing *onomatopoeia*, or "sound words." When your child is on the verge of tears over her toppling tower, you may find that a hearty "Ka*boink!*" from you can send her into a fit of giggles instead. As she gets older, she will try to rebuild the tower, and you can mark her progress with words: "Now another block, then another. Wow! What a tall tower!"

Questions Parents Ask . . .

Q. My ten-month-old tries very hard to say words, but everything comes out "dada." She does change the intonation to resemble the word she's trying to say, but why can't she say words properly?
A. Remember that babies have different ways of entering the world of language. They don't learn everything at once. From what you've said, it sounds as though your baby is focusing on intonation—for now, she is "getting the tune but not the words." Within a few months, you can expect her to get it all together.

Q. My thirteen-month-old used to say "nana" for banana, but now she uses it for everything she wants. Doesn't she realize that everything has its own name? Should I give her what she wants when she asks this way, or will that stop her from bothering to learn the right names of things?

A. Your baby has learned one important concept: that she can use a "word" to get what she wants. She still needs to figure out another important concept: that there are different words for different things. At this point your best bet is to encourage her to use her "word" to communicate, trusting that soon enough she will learn that everything has a name of its own.

Q. Is there any truth to the belief that babies who are early crawlers and walkers will be slow talkers, and vice-versa?

A. While some children do follow either of these patterns, there are plenty who are either early or late at *both* walking and talking. Development is a highly complex, individual affair, but all normal children acquire the skills they need in due time.

Q. My fourteen-month-old spends weekdays with a sitter who has three older children of her own. Lately my child has begun to call the sitter "Mama." She doesn't call *me* that, and it really bothers me, even though I know I have a good relationship with my baby. Why is she doing this?

A. Every mother anxiously waits to hear her baby call her "Mama." When you hear your baby give someone else that honor, it can really hurt! Try to keep in mind that words don't mean quite the same thing to small children as they do to adults. Your little girl is no doubt a keen observer, and has noticed that your sitter answers to the word "Mom" or "Mama" when her three playmates use it. She certainly knows that you are her mother, but she hasn't figured out that "Mama" is a word used only for one's own mother.

If you don't already do so, be sure to refer to yourself as "Mama" or "Mom" as you go about your activities with your baby. And you might ask your sitter to use her own name in the same way during her time with the baby. After a while your child will learn what to call each of you.

FIVE

Sixteen to Twenty-four Months: Vocabulary Explosion

Something extraordinary happens to a child's vocabulary between about eighteen and twenty-four months: it expands so rapidly, and so suddenly, that you might say it "explodes." He may become virtually obsessed with learning the names for things. In a matter of weeks his vocabulary may skyrocket from fewer than fifty words to upwards of several *hundred.* We can get some sense of his excitement by reading a description written by Helen Keller, who learned to speak at a late age because she was blind and deaf. Keller wrote movingly of the day when she held her hand under a water pump and it dawned on her that the word *water* meant "the wonderful cool something that was flowing over my hand. I left the well-house eager to learn. Everything had a name, and each name gave birth to a new thought." Your tod-

107

dler is making a very similar breakthrough
during this period.

Glorious as they are, however, these months
are far from easy for parents. What is often
alarming to adults is the way toddlers use
their newfound verbal ability to express a baf-
fling range of emotions. I regularly receive
desperate phone calls from parents who say
their children have suddenly turned from
easygoing infants into unmanageable toddlers—defiant one minute, and clingy the
next. It can help if you recognize that the difficulties of this period are signs of the enormous growth (both emotional and intellectual)
your child is experiencing. And without a
doubt, one of the most fascinating aspects of
that growth is the toddler's increasingly sophisticated use of words.

Growing and Changing: The Context for Communication

A Social Creature

It's no accident that one way to accuse
someone of being hard to get along with is to
say, "You're acting like a two-year-old!" Don't
be surprised if your child begins to "act like a

two-year-old" around the age of fourteen or fifteen months. He is at times self-assertive to the point of obstinacy, and at times so clingy he bursts into tears if you try to go to the bathroom without his company. While it is not altogether clear why toddlers display these behaviors, many experts believe that they are symptoms of two earthshaking changes in the toddler's life. First, he is beginning to see himself as a separate individual, with motivations of his own. The toddler's natural striving to become more independent gives rise to the nearly constant challenging and obstinacy that are characteristics of this age. This is essentially a healthy, normal part of growing up, but the transition toward greater independence is not an easy one for a toddler to make. Deep down, the child seems to recognize that he is really not ready to take on full-blown independence; he is a small and relatively powerless person in a big, complicated world. According to Dr. Margaret Mahler and her colleagues, the toddler who makes this realization then clings to his mother as a source of safety. During this period the child wants to be in charge, to be powerful, to make decisions; yet he is frightened of the very urges that are pushing him toward independence and forcing him to leave behind the safe world of babyhood. No wonder he can be so hard to live with at times.

Second, throughout these early years the

child has a growing sense of himself as an independent being, but he is beginning to understand that *other* people have goals and motivations of their own as well. According to Dr. Jerome Kagan of Harvard University, at around the age of eighteen months a child begins to become aware of adult standards in many areas of his life. No longer is he happy to sit around for half an hour with applesauce on his chin, or to nibble on biscuits pilfered from the dog's dish. Unfortunately, although he is coming to know that adult standards exist, he has not figured out exactly what they are—which means he may become alarmed by the most apparently insignificant departure from those standards. If your child gets tomato sauce on his shirt at the dinner table, for example, he may demand an immediate change of clothes. If you cut his tuna sandwich in half diagonally instead of crosswise, he refuses to eat lunch. And if he discovers a hairline crack in a plastic car, it's enough to trigger a temper tantrum.

At the same time, he is making increasingly high demands on himself. When he achieves a goal—fitting all the pieces into a favorite puzzle, for example—he will feel the pleasure and pride of accomplishment. But with so much to be learned, and so many skills to be mastered, he is bound to end up frustrated at times. When he is carefully building a block tower, for instance, and it collapses, he invariably collapses, too—in tears.

The toddler's emerging sense of self is nowhere more apparent than on the playground and in the play group. Although he is certainly interested in other children, he is not ready to form what we think of as friendships. Often toddlers engage in "parallel play," or sitting near one another and playing independently with the same kind of toy. Interaction tends to be brief, and often limited to angry shouts of "Mine!" and "Gimme!" which makes constant adult supervision a must. As parents, we need to remember to keep our expectations in line with our children's social abilities, and not to push them to act or feel like idealized adults.

Interestingly enough, at the same time the toddler's burgeoning awareness of the concepts of self and other give rise to occasional displays of *empathy:* one researcher saw a toddler offer his bottle to another child who was crying, in a clear attempt to comfort him. One mother recalls seeing a twenty-two-month-old approach a very angry four-year-old who was sobbing under a table and had refused to be comforted or coaxed out. The toddler was successful where several adults had failed: he jabbered soothingly until the older girl finally emerged from her hiding place.

Making Sense of the World

Your toddler is learning some interesting new approaches to problem-solving. As you may recall, at around twelve months he was discovering that he could work toward a goal—say, standing on tiptoe to reach a plate of cookies. By fourteen or fifteen months he caught on to the trial-and-error strategy: instead of giving up when he can't reach the cookies at first, he tries a different approach (such as pulling on the tablecloth to bring the cookie tray closer). Later, at eighteen to twenty-four months, your child is taking another step forward. Now, rather than actually testing out each possible solution, he can work through some of them in his head and eliminate those that are unlikely to work. This new ability to picture solutions in imagery, instead of in reality, is called *representation*. Let's say your toddler is walking along with a book in one hand and a banana in the other, and decides he wants to open a door. At a younger age, he would have reached out first one full hand, then the other, before arriving at the solution. Now he works out the problem in his head and wastes no time in simply dropping either the book or the banana onto the floor, pulling down on the handle to open the door, then picking up the book or banana again.

The child who can now form mental images, rather than relying on concrete reality for all concepts, also begins to use *symbols* in pretend play. He fills his dump truck with blocks and pushes it around with full sound effects. At some suitable point in the journey, he dumps the blocks with a flourish, and then starts all over again. In these early stages, symbols usually resemble whatever they represent in the child's mind. Later on, however, a stick, a block, or a scrap of paper will "stand for" a car, food, sword, or dish in pretend play. The most important symbols of all, one might argue, are words; language is a system of sound symbols that represent objects, actions, and ideas. For this reason, as we shall see, the child's growing representational ability has a powerful effect on his language development.

Language Learning Now

As we saw in Chapter Four, most children have said their first word by the age of fourteen months, and some will even be able to say ten or more words. By twenty months, they are usually producing "mini-sentences," consisting of two or three words. Language still remains tied to objects that can be seen and touched, however. To offer one example, we know a two-year-old who found her pet

ON AN ERRAND . . .

Outings are a great opportunity to help your child add to his vocabulary. On a Saturday morning grocery run, talk about the food you are choosing ("Now let's get some apples—you can have an apple for lunch. And let's get some spinach. That will make us all big and strong!"). When you stop for gas, you can explain, "We have to get gas to make the car go. See the big thing the man is getting gas from? That's the *pump*. The gas goes through the hose and into our car." Just be sure your child is interested in what you're talking about, and—rather than offering lectures—aim for conversation.

goldfish floating belly-up in the tank. "We're going to say bye-bye to Goldie and bury her," her father told her in a gentle voice. As soon as they got out to the backyard, the little girl ran to the raspberry bushes and stood there waiting patiently. "What are you doing, sweetie?" her father asked. "Goldie's all dead," she replied mournfully. "Berry her." Although such misunderstandings can occur at any age, this child's concrete interpretation of language is typical of the young two-year-old. It is not until the preschool period that children are able to use and understand language that refers to places, times, and actions that are not in the here and now.

Toddlers are not only learning how to put

together words in short sentences. At this age the kinds of words they learn, and the way they use them, are changing in several remarkable ways.

Early Word Use

Why do babies so often say *dada* before *mama?* One at-home mother we know was convinced that her baby had learned to say "dada" first because he saw her as a "mean mommy," since she, as primary caregiver, tended to be less fun than playful Dad. An employed mother, on the other hand, felt "punished" for not being more playful while hurrying to get dinner on the table after a long day at the office. But the most likely reason each baby "honored" his father this way was because "dada" was simply *easier for him to say.* Researchers have found that in babbling, most babies are more likely to produce "da" and "pa" sounds than "ma" sounds. Likewise, when they try to reproduce real words, they naturally say those that are easiest for them to pronounce. Of course, not *all* babies find the same words easiest to say, and as a result they will not all say the same words first. In fact, some will even find "mmm" easier to pronounce than "da" or "pa"—which means they say "mama" first!

Not surprisingly, a baby's early words are

CAUSE AND EFFECT

Does your toddler reach for the light switch every time you carry him through a doorway? Keep in mind at this age he enjoys experimenting with cause and effect. He is learning to associate words such as *on* and *off* with his own actions. Let him switch the light on and off a few times, and describe what is happening ("Turn it *on!* Now turn it *off!*"). Or let him stand at the sink and turn the faucet on and off. You've probably already discovered how much he loves to swing doors to and fro. Feel free to chime in, "Open the door, close the door. Open, close."

---

usually those that refer to things he finds interesting. Anything that moves, for example—*cat, dog,* or *car*—and anything that changes or does something unusual, such as a *light* or *TV.* Everyday objects (*ball, cookie, bottle, shoe*) are also part of the toddler's early vocabulary. The very first word produced by one little boy was "backee," his version of "vacuum cleaner." It marked the beginning of a love affair with the appliance that lasted until he was three years old!

Certain words, such as *more, gone, this,* or *that,* are used over and over again in the course of a day. Obviously, the toddler can use these words (as often as not, to get what he wants) without having to learn specific words for each item. His use of words like *more* and *gone* reflect his new observations about what objects do—that they can disappear and reappear, that they exist even when out of sight. The child who asks for more apple juice, for example, is showing that he realizes the bottle you carried away from the table is now back in the refrigerator.

As your child is expanding his vocabulary, you may notice that he uses some words in a more general way than they are meant to be. Language experts call this *overextension*. Many children, for example, say "mama" not just to call their mothers, but as a way of asking for something from *any* adult who happens to be around. On one occasion, for instance, an eighteen-month-old was holding an orange and standing beside her next-door neighbor. "Mama," she said, holding it out. She clearly wanted the orange peeled, and the neighbor was the best available candidate for the job. Likewise, many children call all four-legged creatures—anything from squirrels to cows—"doggie" or "kitty." Nineteen-month-old Will referred to anything small and round as a "cherry," whether it was a grape, raisin, blueberry, or a marble. And your child may also extend the meaning of a word in order to describe objects of similar texture: a fluffy bath mat or a fuzzy blanket may both be referred to as "kitty," for example.

It is not necessary for a parent or caregiver to correct each and every instance of overextension. After a while the child will begin to narrow his definition of words and use them correctly. As he hears you using a different word for cherry and blueberry, or for dog and cow, he will learn to redefine his own boundaries for those words. And when you do correct him, try to be tactful and encouraging: "Yes, it does look kind of like a doggie! But we call it a cow. See the horns on its head? And see how big it is? And it says 'Mmmooo.' Do doggies say 'Mmmooo'?" The toddler will undoubtedly say no, and perhaps offer a "Ruff-ruff." "That's right!" you might reply. "Cows say 'Mmmooo,' and doggies say 'Ruff-ruff.' " Now, instead of simply telling him he's done something wrong, you've helped him take an active part in learning new information—which will make him more eager than ever to learn to use words.

The Vocabulary Burst

Sometime between eighteen and twenty-four months, you may notice that your child has become almost obsessed with learning the names for things. Many child-language experts believe that this signals an important discovery: the child now knows that *everything has a name.* During this period his spoken vocabulary can shoot up from fifty words to more than several *hundred* in a matter of weeks. By twenty-four months the average child has a vocabulary of more than a hundred and fifty words. Nonetheless, do not be alarmed if your child does not seem to be keeping pace with the statistics. The range among normally developing children is very wide, with some acquiring only fifty or so words even by twenty-four months.

Besides, at this time your child is doing more than just learning new labels for things. Now the *kinds* of words he says and the *way* he uses them change in some important ways. He is beginning to add adjectives and verbs, words that refer to action and that describe objects. Now you begin to hear *dirty* and *broken* (a sign of his concern with adult standards), as well as *hot, pretty,* and *big.* He may pick up a box and make a one-word request: "Open." Riding a trike, he may describe his own action ("Turn").

Another interesting new use of language at this stage is known as the "holophrase," or a single word that implies a whole sentence. He may point to a pair of his father's shoes and say "Daddy." Or he may point to the empty fruit basket on top of the kitchen counter and say, "Banana"—his way of succinctly observing, "Yes, we have no bananas!"

At about this time, most children begin to produce their first word-combinations. Up to now, your child has probably used some two-word phrases, but they were learned as for-

---

NURSERY RHYMES AND ACTION WORDS

"Jack be nimble, Jack be quick, Jack jump over the candlestick!" The two-year-old leaps delightedly over a wooden block. Many children enjoy acting out nursery rhymes this way, and it gives them a chance to listen and relate words to actions. You can do these together. Try acting out "Hickory Dickory Dock," "Little Miss Muffet," "Little Jack Horner," and "Rock-a-bye Baby." Your toddler will also enjoy action songs like "The Wheels on the Bus," "The Eensy-Weensy Spider," and "Bringing Home a Baby Bumblebee."

---

mulas—as far as the child is concerned, they are simply big words. "What's that?" "Do it," "Thank you," and the like are often learned as units, rather than the true combinations of separate words that you may begin to hear now. "Banana poopy! Poopy part!" said one two-year-old in disgust, pointing to the bruised section of her breakfast banana. Clearly, this was no formula but a word-combination she had come up with entirely on her own!

Understanding Words

As you probably realize, toddlers recognize and understand many words that you do not actually hear them say. The average eighteen-month-old can say about fifty words, yet he understands more than two hundred. As always, however, keep in mind that this is only an average—for some children, the gap between production and comprehension is less wide, and for others (especially late speakers) it is wider yet. Although a child's *spoken* vocabulary may be small, it is not unlikely that he understands as many or more words than a child with a large productive vocabulary.

Likewise, a child who overextends a word when speaking (say, by using *doggie* for all four-legged creatures) may be quite capable of pointing to the correct animal when asked, "Do you see a horse?" in a picture book. If you've ever visited a foreign country, you're probably not surprised by this approach; you may recognize the words for *restaurant*, *lunch*, and *dinner* in a foreign language and yet be unable to remember anything but how to ask, "Eat?" when you're feeling hungry.

The Budding Conversationalist

One of the most wonderful developments of this period, at least from a parent's point of view, is the beginning of real conversation between you and your child. He has come a long way since the days when, at six months or so, he let you both ask the questions ("Are you ready to go out and play?") and provide the answers ("Yes," as you tied the strings of his hood, "yes, you are!"). Now, as he puts his doll in a dump truck, and you inquire, "Is baby going for a ride?" he may reply, "Ride!" Conversations with children of this age do not go on very long, of course. Often they are nothing more than your child's simply saying a word or two ("Cookie!") and your reply ("You want a cookie? Well, I think that's okay!"). But by the age of two, he will probably enjoy chatting with you about his favorite topics: cookies (including where they are and how to get them), cars and trucks and dolls. For the time being (and sometimes even beyond the age of three or four), you will be holding up much of the conversation. Nonetheless, these talks will teach your child a great deal about what it means to be a conversation partner—and bring you both a great deal of pleasure in the process.

Everyday Language Learning: How to Help

During this period your child is making dramatic progress. At first having only a vague idea of what language is about, he is rapidly learning to use adult language in conventional, albeit limited ways—most notably, saying words and possibly even mini-sentences. Although these developments are very exciting for both parent and child, it is important not to have overblown expectations once he has begun to produce a few words. You may assume that once he has said his first word that he will quickly learn many more. This rarely happens, however. If you insist that he repeat words when he does not appear inclined to do so, this will do little to facilitate language development.

On the other hand, *naming* things for your child—especially those things that seem to draw his attention most—can be very helpful. "Is teddy smiling?" you might ask, as he looks at a stuffed animal sitting on the rocking chair. Keep in mind that he is interested not only in objects but also in what happens to them. When a bus approaches, for example, you can say, "Here comes the bus," and, after it has passed, "It went away." When the recording you have been listening to comes to an end, you can say, "The music is over." And your toddler will enjoy learning words that refer to his motor activity—"up" and "down," for example, and "jumping" and "running."

Try to use words that are as *specific* as possible. A sentence like "Does Tommy see the ant on the floor?" provides considerably more linguistic information than "Look at that!" Avoid using pronouns as a way of introducing a subject: If your child brings you his doll, it's

> BUBBLES
>
> Blowing bubbles is not only fun, but a great opportunity to talk naturally about some concepts your child is probably very interested in at this point: movement, disappearance, and recurrence, to name a few. "Look! There's a bubble! Look at it fly! Uh-oh! It popped! All gone. Let's make another one. More bubbles! Oh, dear! Now they're gone." Action-packed language "lessons" like this are not easily forgotten.

more helpful to say, "Oh, here's your dolly," rather than "Did you bring him?" And keep in mind that your child is most interested in—and able to respond to—questions and statements about what he is doing *right now*. If he is chasing a ball, the appropriate thing to say is also the most obvious one: "Are you chasing the ball?" This is not the right time to ask if he enjoys having a bath, or singing "The Wheels on the Bus."

Conversation Tips

Helping your child participate in conversation is probably something you do without even realizing it. Whenever he says something ("Ice pop all gone!") and you reply ("Did Jess eat the whole ice pop?"), you are providing a model of adult language as well as offering him the gratifying experience that he has

LAUNDRY AND LANGUAGE LEARNING

Letting your child "help" you sort and fold laundry can turn what you may think of as a humdrum chore that intrudes on your time together into a shared occasion of fun and informal learning. The trick is to talk out loud about motions that you ordinarily do without thinking. "Can Meggie help Daddy fold this towel?" you might ask. Let her hold one end while you fold it. "Can Meggie put it in the basket?" And let her drop it in. Now your child is "learning by doing"; she is hearing new verbs and getting the opportunity to actually perform the actions they describe.

"Whose shirt is this? Is this Mommy's shirt?" you might ask, offering some utterly spontaneous examples of the use of possessives. "Are these Ben's socks? Are these his beautiful red socks?" Let your child reply—either with a "Yeah!" or a smile of recognition, and then supply the words: "Yes, they are his socks. They are Ben's! Let's put them in his pile."

You and your child can enjoy a private joke—and you'll help him learn adjectives referring to size—if you hold up a pair of his pajamas and inquire in a silly voice, "Are these *Daddy's* pajamas?" Wait for a response (a no, perhaps, or some giggles), then answer your own question: "No, they're too *small!* These are David's pajamas!"

STORY-TIME CHATS

At this age your child will enjoy not just hearing a read-aloud story but engaging in conversation about the pictures in the book. At first he will be happy to hear you name them, but after a while, as he begins to learn the labels himself, you can ask, "Where's the dog?" "Which baby is sleeping?" and other questions that help him feel actively involved. Of course, this is not meant to be any sort of test but a chance to spend some pleasurable time together; if he seems puzzled at any of your questions you'll naturally point to the appropriate picture. Perennial favorite books of this age group include Margaret Wise Brown's *Goodnight Moon;* Helen Oxenbury's *Clap Hands, Tickle, Tickle,* and *All Fall Down;* and Eric Hill's *Where's Spot?* and *Spot's First Picnic.*

been understood. As you might expect, this is the best encouragement a child can have.

As you probably learned back on your first date in high school, asking questions is another effective way to keep conversation going. Questions that require a simple yes or no answer are not particularly effective, however; try asking "What?" or "Where?" to offer your child an opportunity to use his developing speech. Let's say your fifteen-month-old is holding a plastic block in his hand, and you know he can name it. "What's that?" you can ask. "Duplo," he will reply. Walking home from the park with a twenty-four-month-old, you can ask, "What did Mommy and Danny do at the park?" and possibly elicit a few responses: "Swing, sandbox, slide."

If your child seems unable to answer, you can boost his confidence by supplying words that help him along. If he does not answer your question about the park, for example, this is a good time to ask a yes or no question: "Did Danny go on the swing?" But do remember to keep your questions about things your child has on his mind. He's still very much interested in the here and now; don't tax his abilities by bringing up topics with which he has little hands-on experience.

However your child tries to communicate— whether in words, gestures, or his own "private" language—be sure your response shows that you appreciate his attempts. It will *not* speed his development if you pretend not to know what he's pointing to, or act as though you are unable to understand his baby talk. Research shows that parents whose children seem to acquire language appropriately tend to avoid correcting them, except in the most tactful ways. If, for example, a child says "Bup" as a bus passes by, you can either focus on his error (by correcting him: "No, say *bus*") or—preferably—reply in a matter-of-fact tone, "Yes, there goes a bus," acknowledging that you have understood him and supplying the correct word.

Likewise, do not try to force language on him. Yours is the exciting task of noticing which words your child is seeking to learn. To try and teach him words for things that may be important to you, or to some textbook child, can only slow him down. For example, you may think it would be wonderful for him to learn color names, or numbers, or to repeatedly tell you his age. Some children are agreeable enough to such performances (especially since they seem to make Mommy and Daddy happy). But they actually contribute little to language development. Why not? Because language growth is inextricably linked to the child's own developing concepts—and he is interested in learning about concepts that loom large in his tiny world. At this stage, and for some time to come, dump trucks and varieties of breakfast cereal may hold considerably more fascination than "higher learning."

Also consider the fact that speaking *with* your child, rather than speaking *to* him, is critical to language development. One way parents can actually impede language development is by focusing too much on using language to direct or control a child's behavior. (Sometimes we have overly high expectations for how "obedient" toddlers ought to be, even though there is research by Dr. H. R. Schaffer of the University of Strathclyde in Glasgow indicating that toddlers tend to comply with adult requests only about *one-quarter* of the time.) Obviously, we need to keep our children safe from harm and to teach them how to feed themselves, use the potty, and so on. But when we spend disproportionately large amounts of time telling them, "Don't put that in your mouth," "Put the doll back on the shelf," and "Stop running," we are probably not leaving much time for talking about whatever is on *their* minds. And as we have seen, children build language by expressing their own interests—which do not, even at this early age, always coincide with ours!

As parents, we can actually hinder language development when our attempts to control our children's behavior, or even to help them learn to speak, threaten to take precedence over the more meaningful exchanges that come from real conversation. But does this mean you should spend every possible minute chatting with your toddler? Not at all. Aside from the fact that you have other things to do, your toddler is busy learning all sorts of lessons from the world around him—how to fit objects into a container, how water feels as he pours it from one cup to another, how to go up and down stairs. You can encourage your child by responding when he speaks to you, and by chatting when it comes naturally as you're getting him dressed, eating meals, and doing errands. Rest assured,

Most parents soon discover that encouraging a child to learn appropriate behavior—rather than constantly criticizing him for misbehaving—is the most effective way to foster self-discipline and responsibility. Happily, this approach is also helpful to language development. Here's a typical example: It's dinnertime, and your child has just dropped her doll on the kitchen floor right between the refrigerator and the stove, where everyone is tripping over it. You might just say, "Pick up the doll!" in an angry tone. Or you can ask, "Is that where dolly belongs? Where does dolly sit during dinner?" and wait for your child to reply. "On the chair!" she is likely to say, and pick up the doll and toddle off to the table with it. Using this approach, you have now encouraged her to use her growing language abilities to *verbalize a rule* and to take responsibility for her prized possession. And the doll is well out of harm's way.

though, that there should be plenty of companionable silence interspersed with your daily talk.

Questions Parents Ask . . .

Q. My eighteen-month-old daughter says a number of words and puts two words together now and then. But she's fairly quiet

compared to one of my neighbor's children who is about the same age. He chatters away, although we can't understand much of what he says. Should I worry that my daughter talks so little?

A. Your daughter is certainly progressing nicely in her language development. The fact that she is less talkative than your neighbor's child may be a matter of temperament; some children, like some adults, talk less than others. You may also be seeing a classic difference in *language-learning* style: your neighbor's child may be a "jargon baby" who is continually practicing intonation patterns. Your daughter, by contrast, is focusing on real words and the way they work in language. She is less likely to speak for the sheer pleasure of hearing the sound of her own voice. But just wait—once she has learned a little more vocabulary and sentence structure, she may turn out to be a real chatterbox!

Q. Why is my seventeen-month-old calling his lambskin comforter "bobbie," which is also his word for *bottle*? He lies on his comforter and has a bottle to go to sleep.

A. Your son has *overextended* the word *bottle* to his lambskin because he associates both of them with comfort and sleep. Children of this age frequently use a word not only for the object to which it conventionally refers, but also for other objects they associate with it.

Q. My twenty-month-old daughter likes to sing while she's playing, and she knows several songs, including her "ABCs." But when I ask her to sing them for someone, she always refuses. Why is she so obstinate?

A. Although some toddlers are willing to "perform" on cue, many are not, and your child's refusals are not at all unusual. At this stage, children are developing a sense of autonomy, and their behavior usually tends toward the spontaneous and self-directed. (Her "obstinacy" is a sign that she's developed a will of her own, which may do a great deal to get her safely through life without caving in to everyone else's demands and expectations.) Try to accept her sense of autonomy, enjoy her songs and her talk when she feels ready to produce them, and avoid trying to stage scenes that do little good for her language development or your relationship.

Q. My sixteen-month-old isn't speaking very much yet, but she loves to play a "pointing game" with us as we look at picture books. She points to each different part of a picture, saying "That" as she points, and she seems to want me to tell her the names of each item. But she never tries to say the words herself. How can I help her do that?

A. You are doing a very good job already. She is telling you exactly what she needs—the names of everything in the pictures—and you are responding appropriately. When she's ready, she will begin to use the words herself. Bear in mind that certain aspects of language learning are controlled by the development of the nervous system. She is undoubtedly learning a great deal right now, and may *understand* quite a few words. As her nervous system matures, she will begin to *produce* them as well.

SIX

Twenty-four to Thirty Months: Learning the Rules

"Don't *want* to!" With these three words, twenty-five-month-old David uttered his very first sentence. It is hard to imagine a more succinct expression of the exciting—and, at times, exasperating—developments that take place in children at this age. As they reach their second birthday most toddlers begin to produce two- or three-word sentences. Alas, those sentences often seem to challenge a caregiver's authority (not to mention her sanity). If your "terrible two" is getting on your nerves, keep in mind that her frequent rebellions are a reflection of her efforts to understand and experiment with rules—rules about sharing toys, using the potty, keeping hands off fragile or dangerous household objects, eating, and sleeping. As you will see, some of the most interesting rules she is coming to learn are those that govern our use of language. Around the second birthday, she will be putting words together into short sentences of two or three words, and during this period she will probably begin to produce four- or five-word sentences. Even though they may not be easily understood by anyone except regular caregivers, these sentences reflect the child's grasp of a number of rules of language, from word order to the use of plurals.

Growing and Changing: The Context for Communication

Making Sense of the World

Over the last few months, your child's thinking has come a long way. Since she turned eighteen months or so, she has been able to find solutions to everyday problems—such as how to reach the cookie jar in the middle of the kitchen table—in her head, rather than by physically testing every possible approach. Now this *representational* thinking ability begins to flower in her pretend play. She can not only pretend to do something herself—say, drink from a cup, brush her teeth, drive a toy car—but she is now able to go one step further away from the physical world, and have a doll or stuffed animal do the "pretending" for her. Now she tenderly tucks her teddy bear into bed, or props up a storybook on the chair beside her. "Shhh, teddy sleeping," she may tell you, or "Teddy reading." These scenes are lovely moments that charm any parent—and also healthy signs that your toddler is progressing, slowly but surely, toward the ability to think and speak about people, objects, and events that are removed from the here and now.

A Social Creature

The child who enjoys "putting teddy to bed" is also revealing a great deal about her growing appreciation of social conventions. She is showing us that she has begun to see herself as part of a social group (her family), with certain rules and procedures. Teddies (and children) sleep in a crib or bed. Books are for reading, not ripping. The toilet paper is not meant to be stuffed in the toilet—or unrolled all the way down the hall. Rules, rules, and more rules! The child is at once burdened and intrigued by them and—as you have probably noticed—she spends a considerable amount of time testing the limits.

Despite her frequent obstinacy, however, she is becoming increasingly concerned with adult standards and with her ability to meet them. So eager are they to live up to these standards that the Harvard psychologist Jerome Kagan has found that children of this age actually get upset when asked to perform a task beyond their ability. When asked to perform a simple act such as "put the hat on the pig" or "hide the stuffed animal under the cloth," children who could not carry out the command became upset and often tearful. Children of this age become very aware of the "correct" way to do things, and can be easily discouraged when they see themselves as unable to do something "right." One twenty-five-month-old girl enjoyed coloring and making small circles on a page with crayon until she saw her college-age baby-sitter make a Valentine card and sign it. "I don't know how to draw," said the toddler in dismay. "I do scribble-scrabble." She refused to pick up a crayon again until her mother reassured her that she was "wonderful" at coloring, at which point she began to fill the pages of a favorite coloring book, singing, "*I* am wonderful coloring!"

In the home or day-care center, a young child is likely to encounter many rules and standards each day (Dr. Kagan reports that a toddler hears an average of nine reprimands per hour!). Although she is doing the best she can to learn to control her impulses, it's not easy. For one thing, she is struggling to grasp the concepts on which many rules depend.

Learning to use the toilet is a case in point. The child needs to understand the ideas of "before" and "after" in order to follow your instructions: "Tell Mommy *before* you poop and we'll go to the potty." (Of course, even a firm grasp of prepositions and verbs is no guarantee of toilet learning: One twenty-eight-month-old girl with a dirty diaper smiled at her mother and proclaimed: "I pooped *before* telling you!")

Another reason your toddler has trouble following rules is that she is still egocentric—not "selfish" in a moralistic sense, but simply unable to see the world from any point of view other than her own. When two-year-old Joey bites his friend Billy, he has no idea that he is producing pain (although he *does* realize that the bite sends Billy running to his mother, leaving the toy behind so that Joey can play with it). It will take many episodes such as this for Joey to learn that his biting can produce undesirable results—the toy's being put away, for example, or the end of the visit.

Although children of this age do enjoy being together, their interactions are still very different from the cooperative play of older children. They primarily engage in *parallel play*—playing side-by-side, but not *with* one another. You will notice that children in this age group only rarely address one another. When one does speak to another, chances are that she will get no reply. What you may notice is that one child offers the other the sincerest form of flattery: imitation. One child picks up a toy telephone, and a few moments later the other finds one of her own and starts dialing. They may even sit back-to-back, calling, "Hello! Hello!" into their phones. But until they are three and a half or four, they are unlikely to engage in pretend play together. For now, social interaction is usually more successful when the toddler plays with an older child or an adult.

Language Learning Now

As with any new development, hearing your child speak in sentences for the first time is a real thrill—especially because it gives a much clearer picture of her view of the world. Her observations are no longer bound by context. Now, rather than being limited to pointing at an object and naming it, she can come upstairs and report an event, such as "Bottle fall down." One twenty-six-month-old, for example, enjoyed watching the neighborhood children board the school bus each morning. "A pool! a pool!" he would shout, and his mother would nod in understanding and say something like, "Yes, the children are getting on the school bus." One morning, after hearing her reply, he drew himself up and looked at her indignantly. *"No,* Mommy," he said, patting himself on the chest. *"My* on a pool." Thanks to this newfound ability to combine words recognizable to his mother into sentences, he was managing to reveal one of his heart's desires. "Unfortunately, once he realized I'd gotten the message," she recalls with a grin, "he assumed we'd ride the bus at that very moment. I spent the rest of the morning with a very frustrated two-year-old!"

Telegraphic Speech

Roger Brown, a psycholinguist at Harvard, coined the term "telegraphic speech" to describe the way young children talk. Like an adult sending a telegram, a child includes only those words that are essential to get the message across. Early sentences are usually no longer than two or three words. "I'm putting my doll in the truck" becomes "Dolly truck." Likewise, "I want Mommy to pick me up" becomes "Mommy up." These short sentences show uncanny awareness of correct English word order. Surprisingly, word-order errors among young children who are learning English are quite rare (although when they do happen on occasion, they are nothing to be alarmed about). They do not say, "Cook Daddy" when they are trying to say that Daddy is cooking. (Comprehension of word order in sentences, however, is quite another matter, as we shall see later on in this chapter.)

Even though her sentences are only two or three words long, the child can often string together several of them to describe action. "Mommy. Blouse on," said one little girl. "Mommy. Skirt on." Although it would be simpler to say, "Mommy, blouse and skirt on," the child has not yet developed such a facility with the language. She is a bit like an adult in a foreign airport, stammering brief phrases in hope they will add up to something meaningful to a passerby ("Bathroom? Woman bathroom? Where?").

Soon enough, your child's vocabulary will include smaller grammatical *morphemes*, or units of meaning, that dramatically increase her ability to get her message across. These include suffixes, or word endings, such as *-er, -est, -ing,* and plural forms.

- The *-ing* form of the verb usually comes first. After saying, "Eat cookie," and "Ride trike," for a while, she will begin to say "eating" and "riding," to indicate that the action is happening now.
- The next grammatical morphemes to appear are usually *in* and *on:* now, instead of saying, "Samantha chair"—which could mean anything from "That is Samantha's chair" to "Samantha is moving the chair"

to "Samantha loves the chair"—she can make herself clear: "Samantha on chair."
* Between now and the time your child turns three, you will probably also hear the plural *-s* (as in "chairs"), irregular past-tense forms ("came," "went," "fell," "broke," "sat," etc.), as well as the articles "a" and "the."

Don't expect your child to use these morphemes in all of her sentences. You will notice that when she is making an effort to say something complicated, she may leave out these morphemes altogether and resort to telegraphic speech. And don't be surprised if your child, after using some irregular forms (such as *mice* and *geese, fell* and *broke*) suddenly begins to say "mouses," "gooses," and "falled" and "breaked." (We will discuss these errors, known as *overregularization,* in the next chapter.)

Questions, Questions, Questions

Your child is beginning to understand how to ask a question. No longer does she do it by simply changing the intonation in her voice as she did at eighteen months ("Cookie?"). Now she is combining words—often incorrectly, however, as in, "Me have cookie?" As she becomes increasingly fascinated with learning the names of things, you will probably hear one question in particular countless times a day: "What dat?" Later on she will be asking "Where?" and finally "Who?" Keep in mind that her use of a particular form of question does not necessarily indicate that she understands what it means; often young children simply appear to ask questions in an effort to keep the conversation going. At this stage her ability to *understand* questions is also still developing. Often around the age of twenty-four months she confuses *why* and *where*. When asked "Why did the boy fall down?" She is likely to answer, "Sidewalk." Within a few months, she will frequently mistake *why* for *what*: Ask her, "Why is the man eating?" and she will respond, "A pickle." Don't be surprised—or discouraged—if your toddler gives a blank stare, or a puzzling answer, to a question. Rest assured that even though she won't understand you every time, the research shows that children respond more often and more relevantly to questions than to any other kind of sentence. Asking your child questions within her linguistic range can help her grow into an active little communicator.

Comprehension

Because your child is learning to talk in leaps and bounds, it is easy to overestimate the amount she can understand. Your child still depends on *context* for clues to help her

ARTISTIC EXPRESSION

Drawing or painting with your child is fun and companionable, and it can give you both plenty to talk about. One father we know, an illustrator by profession, often takes out the crayons and sketch pad to sit down and "draw" with his child, who tends to be reluctant to express his feelings in words. With crayon in hand, he happily depicts his life in lines and circles and then describes his deepest emotions. One day when his mother was away on a business trip, he drew a stick figure. "This is the Mommy," he said gloomily.

"It looks like she's going somewhere," observed his father.

"She is going far far away. To Boston," said the child, who then pointed to a smaller stick figure. "This is her little boy. He's crying."

"Why is he crying?" asked his father.

"Because his Mom went away." Of course, your conversations will not always be so serious, but a child's drawing offers many opportunities for comments and questions. Rather than focusing on the quality of the drawing or making comments like "That doesn't look like an arm," encourage your child to express himself—artistically and verbally—in his own inimitable way.

understand sentences. For this reason, if you are playing with a set of plastic farm animals, she may enthusiastically act out a scene in response to your question "Can a cow chase

---

Cooking

Everyday activities like cooking can be wonderful times for your little one to use language—although there's no doubt you'll need some patience! Make her a "partner" or "helper" by asking her to hand you a carrot, stir up the eggs, or pour the milk. Ask her questions: Which is the biggest spoon? The smallest cup? How do you make a cake? (Her explanation is likely to make you chuckle.) Let her feel that she is making a real contribution to the dinner or snack preparation, and her sense of accomplishment will spur her to talk more and more.

---

a pig?" But when the toys have been put away, the same question may leave her utterly bewildered. And replies to your questions about events removed from the present time, such as yesterday afternoon at the sitter's or tomorrow's trip to the zoo, are likely to be very short indeed—probably no more than a single word.

And despite a child's impressive grasp of English grammar, researchers Robin Chapman and Jon Miller of the University of Wisconsin have found that one of the greatest difficulties she faces at this age is distinguishing the *subject* of a verb from its *object*. To a toddler, two sentences such as "Timmy hit the ball" and "The ball hit Timmy" are likely to mean the same thing (i.e., that Timmy hit the ball), because she is likely to assume that subjects are *animate* and objects *inanimate*. As you are talking with your child, it can be helpful to remember that this kind of mix-up is not at all infrequent.

Conversation?

What do children most like to talk about at this age? You've probably guessed it: themselves. According to psychologist Jerome Kagan, between the ages of twenty-five and twenty-seven months, a full one-third of a child's utterances refer to her own actions— what she is doing, what she wants to do, or what she has done. Because, as we have discussed, this is a time when she is investing a great deal of psychic energy in establishing a sense of self, this is not surprising. "Me do it!" "Ally cookie!" and "It's mine!" are the kinds of short sentences you are most likely to hear, either directly addressed to you or merely as a running commentary while she is playing independently.

Your child is also likely to spend a considerable amount of time repeating what you say. At playtime, for example, you may suggest, "The man can go here, in the truck."

"Truck," your child responds.

"That's right," you reply. "Now he can take a ride! Where will he go?"

"Ride," she answers. "Ride truck."

Sound Game

Your toddler may enjoy a "Guess What I Dropped?" game. Collect a few small objects (keys, a spoon, a plastic cup, an eraser, a pencil, anything you can think of). Let her watch and listen while you drop them one by one. Then have her put her hands over her eyes and guess which object you've dropped by listening to the sound it makes. A favorite variation is switching roles—let her be the "dropper," you the "guesser." (She'll *really* love it if you make some silly, wrong guesses a few times—"Was that an elephant? No? But it made so much noise!")

"Right!" you say. "And where does he want to go in the truck?"

"Truck," she repeats. "Go truck store."

She does not seem to be saying much in this kind of exchange, does she? Yet for many children, repetitive conversations such as these seem to be very valuable for language growth. Dr. Lois Bloom and her colleagues at Columbia University's Teachers College found that some children will imitate *only* those words and forms that they are actually in the process of learning. Apparently, the imitation is not simply a passive process; on the contrary, the child appears to be actively searching for new forms of speech. Not all children imitate in this way, of course. Children who do are, according to some researchers, most likely to have been those who spoke jargon when they were babies.

Interestingly enough, this group of former "jargon babies" is also likely to use pronouns now, saying sentences such as "I do," "Hit it," and "Fit this one here." By contrast, children who were "word babies" and entered language using simple words or object labels rather than jargon now rarely use pronouns and tend instead to refer to themselves and objects by *name*: "Dougie drink," and "Hold dolly." There is absolutely no need to worry that either kind of speech is "immature" or that your child is lacking in vocabulary. Toward the end of the third year, both groups of children gradually begin using nouns or pronouns, whichever form they did not use initially. No matter which pattern your child seems to be following, she is using her conversations with you to learn more about language, and she does it in her own way. She may imitate you, or she may not. She may use pronouns early or late. In any case, her destination is the same. Soon enough, she will have learned all she needs to speak in full sentences.

"ONCE UPON A TIME THERE WAS A CHILD NAMED . . ."

Many children love to hear made-up bedtime stories featuring themselves as the main character. Your little hero or heroine may enjoy hearing action-packed tales—about the time he was invited by the fire chief to ride the hook-and-ladder and ended up saving the day by finding the fire hydrant key. Or he may prefer to join you in recounting the events of his day: "First Bobby got up and ran downstairs," you might begin. "Then he ate the very last . . ." "Banana!" crows Bobby triumphantly.

Everyday Language Learning: How to Help

Everyday opportunities abound to help your child's language flourish during this period. Since she is most fascinated with her own actions, she'll be most likely to respond when you comment on whatever she is doing: "That's a giant apple you're eating!" or "Look at your toes wiggling under the blanket!" She may simply repeat part of what you've said, or she may offer an observation of her own ("Apple big," for instance, or "Apple mine"). Delighted though you are with her exploding vocabulary, there is probably one word you wish she'd never learned: *no*. At times, it seems as though no matter what you ask her she is compelled to answer with a negative. Perhaps you have noticed that often when you ask a question—"Would Michele like a yogurt?"—she immediately replies, "No," and then gets angry if you fail to give her the yogurt. Is there an explanation for this seemingly contrary behavior? Well, researchers have found that at this stage the toddler, who has only begun to understand that a question requires an answer, may say no only because it seems like a suitable reply. She does not really know what it means. This is perfectly obvious if you have ever noticed her saying no to the idea of putting on her jacket—at the same time she is reaching out to put her hand into the sleeve! You can make your own life less frustrating—and help your toddler learn the difference between yes and no—by giving her a second chance to answer when she's responded with a quick no. "Would Michele like a yogurt? Yes or no?" you might ask, holding out the yogurt to her as you say yes, and withdrawing it on the word *no.*

Another conversation pattern you are likely to get caught up in more often than you would like is argument over *ownership.* "*My* truck," says your toddler, struggling to reclaim her toy from a playmate. "Mine! My truck!" It's amazing how quickly a child learns the first-person possessive pronoun *mine,* isn't it? Do not make the all-too-common mistake, however, of assuming that this apparent fluency indicates any deep understanding of the abstract concepts of property. When your child angrily declares, "Mine!" it does little good to explain that the truck belongs to Adam because he got it for his birthday last week. To a toddler, "Mine!" means "I've got it! I want it! Don't try to take it!" Nor is a toddler really able to understand the concept of *sharing*. Telling her, "Nice girls share," is probably more perplexing than enlightening. On the other hand, she may begin to follow directions if you say, "Let's take turns with the truck," or better yet, "First Daniel can have the truck for a few minutes, and then it will be Robert's turn to have it for a few minutes." With experience she will learn to relate certain phrases—"taking turns," "his turn," "your turn"—to ways of behaving that appear to make Mommy or a caregiver happy and also enable her to have *some* time with an alluring toy. And as she matures she will begin to understand such abstract ethical concepts as mutuality and fairness.

There is no need to simplify *all* your language, or to use "telegraphic speech" the way she does, however. Your child will learn much more effectively when you speak adult English and use adult words. There's nothing wrong with the occasional word of "baby talk," but if your child is obsessed with trains, for example, don't limit your conversation to "choo-choo train"—talk to her about the locomotive, the caboose, the refrigerator car, and so on. When a toddler is really interested in a subject, she can learn some surprisingly small details. On the other hand, there's little point in drilling her with labels for things she's not terribly interested in.

How do you know what she *is* interested in? That's simple enough. Just listen to what she says and accept all of her attempts to communicate as expressions of her developing personality. The best way to learn to talk is by talking!

One important way you can encourage her to get plenty of practice is by refraining from correcting her or focusing on her errors. Keep in mind that children make many mistakes as they grapple with the complex system of English grammatical rules and exceptions. Many speech therapists believe that when parents constantly correct a child and focus on the *mechanics* of her speech—such as pronunciation and grammer—rather than on the *message* she is trying to get across, they can actually cause her to develop a stutter. In children between the ages of two and three, some stuttering is perfectly normal. If you ignore it, and make it a point to give your child all the time she needs to say what she wants to say, it will disappear. In the meantime, there's no need to correct her when she proudly calls out, "Me ride trike!" as she's peddling around

TELEPHONE TALKING

Pretending to chat on the telephone with your child is a great way to encourage her to talk. She will probably want a toy phone, but you can try pretending to hold a phone in your hand—or use a block as a pretend phone—while you talk (after a few conversational turns you can continue the game while you fold the laundry, wash the dishes, or paint a chair). "What are you wearing?" you might ask. "What toy do you see in front of you?" As you notice her starting to talk more about events and actions not going on in the immediate present, you can ask what she had for lunch, or what she did outside that morning.

the driveway. The most helpful thing you can do is offer an encouraging answer that shows you share her excitement.

Questions Parents Ask . . .

Q. In one child-care manual I read that the best indicator of a child's intelligence is speech, and that bright children speak early. My twenty-two-month-old daughter is still saying only a few words. Should I be worried that she's not intelligent?
A. Early speakers are *not* the only children who turn out to be intelligent. As mentioned

earlier, Albert Einstein himself was an unusually late speaker! On certain IQ tests designed for older children and adults, performance on the *vocabulary* subsection does seem to correlate with the overall test score. Yet some individuals receive lower scores on that section than they do on the test as a whole, and IQ tells only a small part of the story when it comes to intelligence (see Howard Gardner's book *Frames of Mind*).

There is no reason to suspect any kind of intellectual deficit solely on the basis of your child's relatively late language development. If she does not speak more by the time she is twenty-four months old, however, you may want to consult your pediatrician or a speech and language specialist. For additional information, turn to page 195.

Q. My child speaks beautifully, but his motor skills are below average. My husband is a trial lawyer and I am a teacher. Have we somehow given him the message that language is more important to us than other skills?
A. Why a child develops in any particular pattern is almost impossible to discern. You can be sure that your values and interests are only *part* of the reason that his language is developing so rapidly. Your goals and expectations play a role, but so do your child's own inclinations, abilities, and interests.

If you are concerned that his motor skills are lagging, you may want to spend more time with him on the playground. But don't expect to be able to turn him into a budding gymnast—any more than you could single-handedly have made him into a precocious talker.

Q. My two-year-old seems reluctant to try and say a word until he can pronounce it properly. He won't even say his own name—Christopher—because he can't get it right. We try not to pressure him, but could we be doing something to make him feel insecure about trying to say new words?
A. Children who are frequently corrected when they mispronounce a word may become shy about trying to say new ones. Nor should you tease a child about his mistakes. Simply acknowledge that you have understood by repeating the word as a question, using the correct pronunciation. "I want Ro-ros!" he asks, and you matter-of-factly reply, "Would you like Cheerios?"

Also keep in mind that this is an age when a child becomes highly sensitive to adult standards. Although this awareness is a sign of growth, when he notices that he cannot say a word the way adults say it, he may unfortunately feel frustrated and embarrassed. If you continue to encourage him to talk, he will in all likelihood become less concerned about risking mistakes, or he will eventually develop the motor control he needs to pronounce words correctly.

Q. My two-year-old loves to imitate his best friend's talking—including his friend's mispronunciations. Is this bad for my child's language development?
A. Don't worry. The fact that your child can imitate his friend's sounds so well is in itself a testimony to his control over pronunciation. Eventually he (and his friend) will follow adult models and learn to pronounce words the way adults do.

Q. My twenty-three-month-old daughter is very verbal, but sometimes I wonder if she really *understands* the words she says. She's been saying the word *yesterday* a lot lately, but as often as not she's using it incorrectly—instead of "last week," or even "tomorrow."
A. You've noticed a very interesting fact about language development. Children do indeed say things they don't fully understand. But this does not mean they are not learning. On the contrary, by practicing a word they learn to refine their use of it. Although your daughter's use of the word *yesterday* may be incorrect much of the time, she does use it to refer to some aspect of *time*. So she has a sense of the word's meaning already. By using it, and by getting feedback from you (when you say,

for example, "Yes, we will go to Grandma's tomorrow. We went to Burger King yesterday"), she will slowly learn what *yesterday* means.

Q. My child-care person is very gentle with my child, and responsible, but *very* quiet. She doesn't talk a lot or make up stories for her. My child does have lots of interaction with other children on play dates, though. Should I worry?

A. How *much* your caregiver says to your child is less important than how good she is at making what she says count—for your child. Does she speak to your child about events and things that seem to be important to her? Or does what she says seem to be not only limited in quantity, but in quality as well? Does your child appear happy to be with her or is she fussy and bored? As for the play dates, although kids learn a great deal from peer play, *basic* language skills at this age are learned from loving adults.

Q. My husband tries to talk to our two-year-old girl about things she doesn't have much interest in—like baseball games on TV. Although she loves playing with her dad, so much of what he says seems to go over her head that I'm concerned she's not really learning anything from interacting with him.

A. Although it is important to follow the child's lead in language as well as play, research has shown that fathers do interact differently with their children than do mothers. Although they may aim a bit too high over the child's level, fathers often seem to present challenges that inspire the child to move ahead. (Mothers, for whatever reason, are generally more sensitive to the child's current developmental level.) Although the research is inconclusive about these differences in style, I think we can assume that *both* kinds of interaction help a child develop. A child will show you when something is really *too* far off-target by simply tuning out. But since your daughter enjoys playing with her father, her time with him is undoubtedly contributing not only to her language development, but to her emotional growth as well.

Q. I notice in the day-care center that the adults don't have much time to individually talk to the children. Is my child missing out on important opportunities to learn?
A. Young children definitely need a great deal of one-on-one time with an adult for optimal development in all areas. Good day-care staff are sensitive to these needs, and make it a point to speak with each child at frequent intervals. If there seems to be too little individual attention in your child's class, you might discuss your concern with her teacher and the center's director. They should be sensitive to your concern and willing to discuss how they might improve the situation.

SEVEN

Thirty to Thirty-six Months: Language As a Learning Tool

Michael and his mother are making cookies in various shapes. "What's that one?" asks Michael, pointing to a cookie cutter.

"That's the pumpkin," his mother replies. "We made pumpkin cookies at Halloween, remember?"

Michael responds with a favorite question: "Why?"

"Because it was Halloween," answers his mother, "and pumpkins are for Halloween. Aunt Sarah gave you that cookie cutter when you were sick."

"Why did I be sick?" Michael asks quickly.

"Well," says his mother, "you caught the flu."

"Why?" asks Michael once more.

"Well, I'm not sure," says Mom, growing slightly impatient. "You probably caught it from another child in school."

But Michael won't give up: "Why did I caught it?"

You're probably very familiar with this pattern of conversation if your child is a preschooler. At this stage, a child's use of *why* reflects his growing ability to use language as a tool to help him learn about the world around him. Although he still makes grammatical errors (such as "Why did I be sick?"), he is now capable of speaking in longer sentences that are far more complete than those the "telegraphic" speaker can manage. And although most of his talk is still in the here and now, he can refer to events out of the current context. How much he has learned in a very short time! No wonder the Soviet scholar and poet Kornei Chukovsky wrote in his classic book *From Two to Five* (1968):

It is frightening to think what an enormous number of grammatical forms are poured over the poor head of the young child. . . . If an adult had to master so many grammatical rules within so short a time, his head would surely burst—a mass of rules mastered so lightly and so freely by the two-year-old "linguist". . . . In truth, the young child is the hardest mental toiler on our planet. Fortunately, he does not even suspect this.

Although the three-year-old still has much to learn, he has become adept enough with lan-

guage that he can use it to learn more about
the world. New words introduce him to new
ideas. Language is also an important part of
his social life; he is learning to share not only
toys but ideas with his friends as they enjoy
fantasy play. In spite of his obvious limitations, he is a rather impressive little conversationalist.

Growing and Changing: The Context for Communication

Making Sense of the World

At this stage, the child is still egocentric,
and his self-centered world view is reflected
in the way he thinks about events. In what
has been called "magical thinking," he firmly
believes that his own thoughts and wishes
can *cause* changes in the world around him—
often on a grand scale. For example, he may believe that the sun comes up because he opens
his eyes in the morning, or that the moon
comes out so that he can see in the dark.
Sometimes his interpretations can even upset
him. He may think lightning struck the electrical wiring and made the lights go out because *he* was bad. Or, sadly, that Mommy and

Daddy are getting a divorce because *he* refused to let Daddy give him a bath.

Until the age of six or seven, he will often tend to attribute intentions, wishes, feelings, and even actions to inanimate objects, a way of thinking known as "animism." One child of three asked his father why the stars twinkle, and then announced that he already knew the answer: "They twinkle when they whisper secrets to one another!" Another child described rainy days as sad, "because the clouds are crying." And another three-year-old explained that lightning bugs light up because "they're afraid of the dark."

In the three-year-old's mind, an inanimate object may even try to hurt him on purpose. Don't be surprised if your child concludes that his roller skates are bad because they tripped him, or that the table is "mean" because it bumped his head! One four-year-old demanded that his favorite toy—a large metal fire truck—be banished to the basement, because "it cutted me on the hand."

A child's thinking is less cohesive than you might expect at this age, flitting from one idea to the next with no apparent rhyme or reason. He seems to string together random thoughts in stream-of-consciousness fashion. "Once upon a time a monkey was walking on the forest," began a three-year-old boy. "And he just jumped out the tree. 'Cause he got all covered up. 'Cause it was snowing all day. 'Cause it was snowing all day, and it was also even do-ing . . . something." Rather than building to-ward a climax in any sort of ordered way, the thoughts in this "story" are strung together like beads on a string. What is the connection between the monkey and the snow? The idea of being "covered up" seems to have brought snow to the child's mind. In the end, he loses his train of thought altogether.

It is the imagination that is beginning to flower. This is a time when children begin to assume pretend roles—clunking around in Daddy's shoes and trying to repair the dish-washer with a wrench, for example. By the age of three, a child may spend long periods of time "in character." He begins by pretend-ing to be Daddy, the doctor, or the mail car-rier, and then expands his role-play to characters that capture his sense of adven-ture—firefighter, knight, or racing driver. He really *believes* that he is his favorite super-hero: of course he can't wear a winter jacket over his Superman costume—after all, Super-man never does.

The props a child uses in pretend play offer fascinating insights into his cognitive devel-opment. The three-year-old firefighter makes a "hose" out of a stick—or, better yet, an empty wrapping-paper roll—and puts out fires all over the house. Unlike the two-year-old, he doesn't need a real hose to carry out his game. Within a year or two, even the nonrealistic props will be dispensable (although he will still enjoy using them). The four- or five-year-old can do lots of pretending with no more equipment than words and imagination. In fact, as the child gets older, words become an increasingly essential part of his play. We know he is pretending to be a cowboy not so much because he is wearing his father's old hat, but because he *tells* us: "Bang! Bang! I'm a cowboy in the Wild West! Watch out, I'm looking for the bad guys!" Like his language, his play has become increasingly *decontextualized*, or less tied to the concrete reality of the physical world.

A Social Creature

Have you noticed your child becoming more and more interested in the concept of gender identity? "I'm not wearing that shirt," he announces in disgust, pointing to a narrow stripe across the chest. "See? It has *pink* on it." He is coming to realize that some people are boys or men, and others girls or women, and to understand which he is. Although your child will probably know whether he is a boy (or whether she is a girl) by thirty-six months, the concept of gender identity does not seem to stabilize until the age of six or seven.

In the meantime, however, sex-role stereotypes can be surprisingly intense. A preschooler tends to interpret any behavior not consistent with sex-role stereotypes as "bad." A boy may not want girls at his birthday party, a girl may refuse to wear pants, and neither may think Mom should wear Dad's pajama top. The late developmental theorist Lawrence Kohlberg of Harvard explained the extreme sex-stereotyping that is typical of preschoolers as the result of the child's trying to make sense of the world. When a child is learning a "rule" for how things are supposed to work, he tends to be very rigid about its application in every single instance. (This is also true with language, as we shall discuss later on in this chapter.) If he has observed that necklaces are worn by girls and women, for example, he is likely to refuse to wear anything resembling one around his own neck— even as part of an Indian costume on Halloween. There is no need to worry about the extremes to which your three-year-old may take his sex role, or to wonder how he picked up such stereotypes in spite of your best efforts to avoid "gender bias." By the age of six or seven, when he feels comfortable with the rules he has learned, he will lighten up a bit.

Language Learning Now

The Preschool Poet

By the age of three, most children can say approximately a thousand words, and many are saying more. Impressive as this sounds, the child is continually adding new words. Toward the end of this period, he begins to understand that a single word can have more than one meaning—that *funny* can mean "amusing" or "strange," for example, and that the word *plant* could refer either to a philodendron or a factory. But for the most part, he will only learn the most common, concrete meanings of words that can be experienced through the senses. If he overhears you gossiping about an acquaintance you find "cold," for instance, he may ask, "Why doesn't she wear a sweater?" He is likely to outright reject everyday adult metaphors as "silly" or just plain wrong. "A book doesn't have a jacket, you silly mommy!" said one three-year-old condescendingly.

But this does not mean his language is dull or uninventive. On the contrary, he is apt to be highly creative with words. Now that he understands that words and phrases are used to refer to objects and ideas, he feels free to make up his own when necessary. One boy who had been warned not to eat turkey bones at Thanksgiving dinner, for example, later refused to eat the crust of his pumpkin pie. "It's the pie bone," he explained. Another described a collection of rocks that had been found at the edge of a river as "musical rocks," because "the river rolls them and rolls them until they learn to sing." Still another child rejected his eggplant Parmesan dinner, complaining, "This stuff is too *bluffy.*" Isn't it amazing the way the two- or three-year-old's invented words so often manage to express their intended meaning?

Toward the end of the third year, your child will begin to reveal an awareness of some important and rather abstract concepts. Although most of his talk still refers to events in the here and now, through fantasy play he is beginning to use *decontextualized language,* or to talk of things far removed from him in time and space. Now, instead of simply describing what he is doing as he did a year ago ("I eating Cheerios"), he shares a fantasy: "I'm flying the airplane. Now we're going to land!" As he does this, he uses the past tense with understanding ("I splashed in the pool," "I played with Roger"), and even makes some references to the future—"I'm gonna build a sand castle," or "I'm gonna eat at Pizza Hut."

You may also notice him referring to *time* and *duration.* "I take a nap last year yesterday ago," said one boy. "Mommy," begged a

---

DRESS-UP

A box filled with dress-up clothes is an excellent way to encourage fantasy play, and your child will be especially eager to learn new words and ideas that help bring his or her favorite pretend character to life—"briefcase," "siren," and "high heels," for example. Instead of discarding your old shoes, jewelry, and jackets, let your boy or girl enjoy putting them on and tripping around the house "playing Mom," or policeman, or teacher. An assortment of hats is also a great spur to the imagination. Check for low-priced toy fire hats and cowboy hats in a dime store or resale shop.

---

little girl as her mother dropped her off at nursery school, "will you stay with me for a few whiles?" He may progress beyond demanding "More!" to a more sophisticated understanding of *quantity.* "I ate ten thousand hundred million potato chips at Daniel's house!" And he is developing a notion of *distance.* "Grandma's house far away—two hundred *pounds* away!" As you have probably observed, he does not really grasp the specific meaning of the words and phrases he now uses as units of measure, but his use of them shows that his view of the world is expanding, and he is doing his best to express his new ideas.

Causality

Research by the child-language specialists Lois Hood and Lois Bloom of Columbia University has shown that children begin to talk about causality very early, in some cases before the age of two and a half. In doing so, however, they do not use "connective" words like "because" or "so." Instead, they simply juxtapose two related sentences: "Man fall off table. I push him." The two sentences may be arranged in order of cause and effect ("I dropped my banana. It broke.") or effect and cause ("My banana broke. I dropped it.").

For many children, *and* is the first connective to be used, as in "My ice cream melt and fall on my shirt." But interestingly enough, as they begin to use *so* or *because,* children seem to divide into two different groups. Researchers Hood and Bloom have observed that children who first used *cause-and-effect* word order in their early statements of causality as children begin to use *so* first, progressing from "Michael hit me. I hit him." to "Michael hit me so I hit him." Children who go on to use *because* first are those who earlier used *effect-and-cause* word order; they begin saying, "I hit Michael. He hit me," and later say, "I hit Michael because he hit me." This may seem like a fine point, an observation of academic interest only to child-development experts. But in reality, this example of individual variation helps us understand that there is *no one way* to learn language. All children eventually learn to use both *because* and *so*, of course, as well as other words that indicate causality—*if, when,* and *unless.* But there are many different paths on the way to language development. Most of the variations mentioned in this book have been observed only in recent years, and many more are likely to be discovered in the years to come. When you're tempted to compare your child's language development with that of his favorite nursery-school buddy or the little girl down the street, keeping that in mind can be very reassuring.

Why, Why, Why

Children begin to ask "Why?" at around the age of two and a half, and once they start you hear more *whys* a day than you might have ever imagined possible. At every turn, your most insignificant observation is questioned. You feel as though you are being continually cross-examined. "Let's get into the car and go to the store," you tell your three-year-old.

"Why?" she asks.

"Because we need food," you answer, holding out her jacket.

"Why?" she asks again.

"Because we want to be big and strong,"

you respond, helping her put her arm into the sleeve.

"Why we want to be big and strong?" she asks.

"So that we can be healthy," you reply, getting more than a bit impatient.

And there she goes again: "Why?"

"So we don't get sick!" you say in exasperation. "Now get into the car!"

One reason the constant stream of *whys* is so difficult is that although you realize you could never provide a satisfactory answer to each *why*, you want to encourage your child's curiosity about the world and may even feel guilty about ignoring or refusing to answer the question. You may even feel inadequate because, like every parent, you find it difficult to answer many or your child's *why* questions: "Why is the sky blue?" "Why are there poor people?" "Why did Jamie's grandma die?" It may help to keep in mind that when your child asks "Why?" he is not necessarily using the word as precisely as an adult speaker. He may simply be using it as a device to keep the conversation going, especially at the end of the day when he is tired and lacks the energy to say anything more complicated (but doesn't want to give up). At any hour of the day, although he is eager for information about the way things are and how they have come to be, keep in mind that he will not understand the kinds of abstract explanations you may think he is demanding. Some *whys*, in other words, are impossible to answer.

One dad says he heads off each impossible *why* with a silly response. "Why do I have to wear my jammies?" "Because you might scare the giraffe if you don't." And a mother we know found it helpful to think of each of her son's *whys* as "tell me more." Rather than trying to *explain* every aspect of reality about which her son asked, she made an effort to help him connect it to other people, places, and concepts with which he was already familiar. For example, when he asked, "Why doesn't that man have a house to live in?" she explained, "Because he has no job and no money," and then, when another "Why?" inevitably followed, she said, "I don't know. I hope the man will get something to eat at the soup kitchen where you and Daddy help out."

Pronunciation

Even at this age, many children are making some pronunciation errors. A two-and-a-half- or three-year-old will often *omit* certain sounds (*'poon* for *spoon*, *'brella* for *umbrella*, and so on) or substitute one sound for another (*wabbit* for *rabbit*, *tiss* for *kiss*). He may also distort certain sounds, saying *mouze* for *mouse,* for example. And he may continue to pronounce incorrectly some of the words he learned in his earliest talking days; one boy who learned to say "lawn mo-mo" for "lawn mower" at eighteen months, for instance, kept pronouncing it that way until he was four years old.

Most parents realize that pronunciation errors are a normal part of language development, but they often do not realize how long errors can persist. Between the ages of three and three and a half, most children have mastered all the vowel sounds and some of the consonants. But even by the age of seven, some perfectly normal children will make errors with the more difficult sounds, especially *consonant blends* such as *st (steak), sk (skate), gl (glide), sn (snow),* and *pl (play).*

Keep in mind that your child often cannot *hear* (much less correct) his own pronunciation errors. If you point out a mistake, he may deny indignantly—repeating the error in his denial! In Samuel Butler's *The Way of All Flesh* (1903), for example, a small boy named Ernest tries to sing a favorite hymn entitled "Come, Come, Come; Come to The Sunset Tree for the Day Is Past and Gone," and was unable to say anything but "Tum, tum, tum." When sternly instructed to say *come* "like other people," he replies innocently, "I do say tum." (His father, calling him "self-willed and naughty," punishes him harshly.)

To cite a contemporary example, we know one three-year-old who asked his mother, "Where are my wings?" She managed to locate the angel wings he had recently worn in their church's Christmas pageant, and she gave them to him. "Those aren't my wings—they're my *wings*," the little boy protested.

"Well, which wings did you want?" asked his puzzled mother.

"Not *wings*, silly—my *wings!* The wings I got at Wobert's party!" Now his mother understood that he was asking for the *rings* he had brought home as a party favor from a friend's birthday celebration! (And unlike the Samuel Butler character, she laughed heartily and hugged her little boy.) Some researchers believe that children are focusing on what they want to say, rather than listening to the words they have actually pronounced. In any case, it is clear that most children who make such errors simply cannot do any better for the time being. A wise parent models the correct pronunciation while being careful to avoid humiliating the child, even inadvertently.

Other Common Mistakes

Children between the ages of two and four frequently use *pronouns* incorrectly. This is hardly surprising when you stop to consider how complicated using pronouns really is. For one thing, the meaning of a pronoun can change; *you* and *I* are words that refer to different people, depending on who is speaking. Then there are the different pronoun forms that refer to the *same* person or thing: the child needs to learn that we say, "Bob gave *him* the book," but *"He* gave the book to Bob." As your child is sorting out these rules, you are likely to hear errors. The child may say, "Him hitted me," "I want she dolly," "My go outside," and so on. Shortly after his third birthday, one little boy confused *I* and *you* for several weeks: "Mommy, sit on my lap," and "Daddy, can you eat that candy bar now?" Needless to say, his parents were somewhat bewildered until they caught on to the erroneous pattern!

Irregular verbs and plurals are also tricky. You may be surprised to notice that your child is using certain irregular forms correctly: two-year-olds are capable of learning *mice, men,* and *geese,* even though they do not follow the general English plural form (adding -*s).* Likewise, they can pick up such irregular past-tense verbs as *broke* and *found.* But now that your child is three, you may be sitting in the park one day and suddenly hear your child exclaim, "Mommy, let's feed the *gooses!"* And then, as he chases them, "Look! They *flied* away!" Why, you wonder, is he suddenly making mistakes when he knew irregular forms so well when he was younger? You're sure that *you* never make such mistakes, and you've carefully checked that he is hearing correct English from the baby-sitter. Where, then, is he picking up these erroneous forms?

Rest assured that your child isn't the first to make these mistakes. In fact, the good news is that it would only be worrying if he *weren't* making them. Researchers now believe that a preschooler's attempts to regularize irregular verbs and plural forms are evidence that he is *actively analyzing the rule system* of the English language. In his zeal to follow the rules he is learning, he applies them in every instance in which they logically *should* be used. You can help him by simply repeating whatever he's said—without placing too much emphasis on his error—and using the correct form. "We made a bird feeder and we feeded the birds!" he may tell you after an afternoon at the sitter's. And you might reply, "Oh, you fed the birds? That's exciting! Were they gobbling the food?" By the time he is six or seven, he will have heard the correct (irregular) forms often enough to master the language, exceptions and all.

Conversation

Although your child can now participate in fairly long conversations with you and other adults, your patience and support are still necessary because he is by no means a skilled conversationalist at this point. For one thing, his egocentricity leads him to believe that everyone knows exactly what is on his mind. This can lead to some bewildering omissions. One two-and-a-half-year-old girl recently announced to a neighbor, "I'm gonna go do it now," and walked out her front door. What was she going to do? "Go home and play with my doll," she explained, as though the answer were obvious. (The doll in question had been discussed some twenty minutes earlier.) Neglecting to let the listener in on the topic of his proposed conversation is very common with the two- or three-year-old, and even a four-year-old (especially when upset or tired) can appear to be talking in riddles. One preschooler arrived home from nursery school and declared he was *never* going back "because he wouldn't let me even though I said I would." It took some coaxing from his mother to learn that he was recounting a dispute over which child would be the policeman and which the robber in a playground fantasy!

As for conversations with other children his own age, the two- or three-year-old is still very limited. After all, children can't help each other keep a conversation on track the way adults can! It is not until the age of three and a half or four that conversations between children get longer and more focused. Most often, the focus is a fantasy situation. "Let's be fire-fighters!" they begin in a burst of enthusiasm. Don't be surprised, however, if they reach an impasse: "This is a hook-and-ladder truck!" "No, it's a pumper!" At this age, egocentrism is still very strong, and cooperation is no mean feat.

Everyday Language Learning: How to Help

Now that your child has a good basic *vocabulary,* you can help him continue to learn new words by providing him with new ones when you see him searching for them, and especially offering synonyms for the words he already uses. If he grumbles that he "be mad at Lisa," for example, you might reply, "Oh, you say you're angry at Lisa?" Naturally, there is no need to force yourself into such responses or to consciously supply him with a fresh synonym every time he speaks. When the occasion arises, however, this technique can be helpful. It is especially useful to help him learn adjectives; when he uses simple words such as *big,* you can offer a more precise term—"Yes, it's *tall,*" or "Look how *high* the tower is," or "That is a *fat* plum." Although the generalized descriptors will not disappear from his vocabulary, you will be providing him with the rich language he needs as a model for the time when he is *ready to learn* these fine distinctions.

You have probably noticed that he is ready to express much more than he could in his early, telegraphic speech. Now he wants to talk about why things happen, how, and with what equipment. You can help him with the *grammatical* information he needs to express his increasingly complex ideas. At first he will do so rather haltingly, in series of short sentences: "I put jacket on. Cold outside." At this stage you can help by putting it all together in a single sentence: "Yes, you need your jacket because it's cold outside."

As he reaches for more complex syntax, he will be paying a great deal of attention to the verb structure of *your* sentences. If you say, "Before we go outside we need to pick up the blocks," he is likely to reply by using your verb: "Pick up the train set, too." This is his natural way of practicing syntax. It is a "learning system" that is natural, active, and dependent on live interaction. One mother who was concerned that her two-year-old's speech was lagging mentioned the problem to her neighbor. "Why don't you have him watch more 'Sesame Street'?'' the neighbor recommended. Keep in mind that no matter how good the television show, it cannot provide your child with the interactive learning offered by a live adult like Mom, Dad, or a familiar caregiver.

Sometimes you may notice an opportunity to help him *build sentences.* If, for example, he sees you putting on your hat and coat and observes, "Mommy going bye-bye," you might respond, "Yes, Mommy is going to the store," and hear him say, "Mommy go bye-bye store."

Conversation and Courtesy

Have you noticed that the above suggestions all occur in the context of everyday conversations? Keep in mind that this is how most language learning occurs. Special "teaching" sessions or flash cards are unnecessary, and even the best of television programs is no substitute for real, live conversation.

One way conversation helps is to teach the child to use language appropriately in different social contexts. As we pointed out at the beginning of this book, language learning is much more than acquiring words and grammar. The child must learn what to say when. He will learn to be courteous not because you

---

PUPPETS

Trying on different roles—Daddy, a lion, a clown, a monster—by playing with puppets can be great fun for a young child. Your child will practice the language he thinks is appropriate to his character—and vary the pitch of his voice according to each role, too! Look for simple hand puppets (some can double as washcloths for bath-time use) or inexpensive finger puppets. And, of course, you can make your own paper-bag puppets by drawing eyes and hair on the bottom of a brown paper sandwich bag. You can get him started by showing him how to hold the puppet and "make it talk" and starting a simple dialogue between your puppet and his. But he'll also be perfectly happy to talk *to* his puppet, Charlie McCarthy–style. For this reason, there is no need to worry about a puppet stage.

---

drill him with rules of etiquette, but because you are courteous to him. Because he is still egocentric, it is not realistic to expect spontaneous use of *Please* and *Thank you* until he is four or five. Then, thanks to your good examples, one day he may pleasantly surprise you, as a kindergartner did one Halloween, by ringing a neighbor's doorbell and calling out, "Trick or treat—please!"

Reading Aloud

Now that your child can not only point at and name the illustrations in a book but actually sit and listen to a story, reading aloud is an opportunity for him to begin to comment—in rudimentary, but often surprisingly insightful ways—on plot and character development. If, for example, you are reading Maurice Sendak's *Where the Wild Things Are,* you might ask your child, "How do you think Max felt when his mommy sent him to bed without anything to eat?" In this way you are helping your child to reflect on the events in the story and express his observations in words. He is building a *vocabulary.* He is learning to be a good *listener,* a critical role in the communication process. These are invaluable skills for the everyday use of language, and especially for *reading comprehension* later on, when he starts school.

Questions Parents Ask . . .

Q. Is it true that firstborn children learn to speak earlier than second children?
A. This does seem to be a general trend, but *only* a general trend. I have heard mothers of late-talking second-borns sometimes worry

---

READING TOGETHER

Encourage your child to take an active part in story-time by choosing books that make it easy for him to "chime in." Books with a pronounced rhythm and rhyme, like Dr. Seuss' *Green Eggs and Ham*, lend themselves to "joint reading" ("Would you like them in a house? Would you like them with a . . . mouse?"). Nursery rhymes are always popular, as is almost any book your child has heard frequently enough to learn the words.

---

that the second gets less attention, or the first doesn't give the younger one a chance to speak. On the other hand, I've heard mothers of second-born children who are *early* talkers explain, "Well, it's only natural, because she learns so much from her older brother!" Whatever the reason, keep in mind that there is *no* evidence that later-born children are at any linguistic disadvantage later in life.

Q. Whenever my child uses an incorrect consonant at the beginning of a word—like "tookie" for *cookie*, I correct him. I say, "No, not *tookie* with a *t, cookie* with a *c.*" I think this will help him sound out words later, when he starts to read. Is there any harm in this?

A. A great deal depends on the specific context in which you do this—what your child is like, how often you do it, your tone of voice and manner when you correct him. This approach may fit in perfectly well with your relationship. But if you correct him too frequently, or if he is very sensitive, you may be undermining his confidence. Since there is little evidence that teaching him the link between letters and sounds is effective at this point, you would do more for his reading readiness by including nursery rhymes and poems in your story-time, and by playing word games.

Q. Our child's caregiver, who comes to our home each day, is very warm and caring. But lately I've begun to worry that her heavy foreign accent will be a hindrance to his language development. Will he have trouble understanding her, or will he speak with a foreign accent?

A. As long as your caregiver does speak English, your child will have little trouble understanding her, especially because most of their conversation is likely to be about things that are going on in the present.

Your child is not likely to develop a foreign accent. Your caregiver is only one language model, and—given the special nature of the parent-child relationship—your child will tend to focus more on your language patterns than on those of anyone else. Don't be disturbed, though, if he does say a *few* words with a foreign accent!

Q. My three-year-old loves TV and watches from morning till night. I'm careful to restrict his viewing to educational programs. But I've heard it said that TV can interfere with language development. Is this true?

A. There is good evidence to show that TV is not a sufficient source of language input to teach children to talk. The occasional new word they learn from TV is small change, compared to what they learn from participating in conversations with sensitive, interested adults. No matter how high the quality, the amount of TV your child is watching is excessive.

Q. My two-and-a-half-year-old isn't speaking very well yet. But he is learning *two* languages, French and English. Could this account for his slow rate of language development?

A. Children in bilingual homes often acquire both languages a bit more slowly than monolingual children at first. And during this early period, don't be surprised to hear your child produce sentences that include words from both languages. It takes a while for the child to realize that the two languages are separate systems. By the time they are three, most bilingual children do begin to distinguish words in one language from those in the other, but it takes longer for them to keep the grammatical features of the two languages distinct; the child uses one set of grammatical rules for both languages. Your French-speaking child, for example, may use double-negatives in English. But by the time he is four, he will probably have caught up in his language skills—in both French and English. You can minimize his confusion by making sure he hears each language consistently from the same person; for example, if your spouse is a native speaker of French, he should speak French *exclusively* with your child, and if you are an English speaker you should avoid slipping from French to English and back again.

APPENDIX

※

Potential Problems and How to Spot Them

It's perfectly natural for a parent to worry at times about a child's mispronunciations and other language mistakes. "The way he talks can be cute and funny, but will he outgrow it?" you may wonder. Fortunately—as we have shown throughout the pages of this book—the vast majority of errors do disappear in the course of normal development. Most children learn to speak with a fluency and charm that amazes scholars and parents alike. But in a few cases—approximately six percent of children—warning signs of potential language problems show up even at this early age. A toddler may not attain important language milestones, for example. A preschooler's pronunciation errors may be so severe that he cannot be understood. Or a child who has had repeated ear infections may have trouble hearing sounds and, consequently, be unable to reproduce them.

There is a variety of possible reasons for a lag in a child's language growth. Sometimes the problem may be part of a general developmental delay. It may be that the child's linguistic environment is insufficiently rich or stimulating. The language difficulty may be a sign of damage to the nervous system. And in extremely rare cases, the language problem may be accompanied by other symptoms that suggest an emotional disorder.

If your child does not appear to be acquiring language as he should, it is wise to discuss the problem with your pediatrician. In this chapter we will discuss in detail three of the most common problems found in young children: *hearing impairment*, which if left untreated can result in language delay; *articulation problems*, or severe errors of pronunciation that can eventually have a negative impact on a child's social development and reading and writing skills; and *language delay*, which can slowly turn into language disorder. Should you suspect a hearing impairment, the pediatrician is likely to recommend having the child's hearing checked. In the case of an *articulation problem* or *language delay*, you should consider having your child evaluated by a speech and language pathologist. Fortunately, the earlier these difficulties are detected and treated, the better your child's chances for improvement will be.

Hearing Problems

Twenty-four-month-old Jason and his mother, Mary Ann, are walking into the playroom of a child-development laboratory for an observation session. Jason is running from one toy to another, taking a brief look at each one and then tossing it aside as he runs to the next. There is nothing particularly odd about this behavior in itself. As the minutes go by, however, Jason does not appear to be settling down and focusing the way most children would at this age. He continues to run around the room frenetically, picking up toys and glancing at them, but he seems unable to become absorbed in anything, and each toy is quickly discarded. No matter how hard his mother tries to entice him to play—by holding up a toy, and even by getting down on her hands and knees and pretending to be a dog—he quickly tires of her suggestions, only to resume rushing from one end of the room to the other.

After the session is over, Mary Ann voices her concern about her son. "He started talking at fourteen months—he could say about ten words at that point," she recalls. "Then all of a sudden he stopped adding new words and didn't even seem to be using his original ten!" Although he was still vocalizing quite a bit, his words had a strange, garbled sound. "I've tried everything I can think of to get him to talk, but I'm not getting anywhere," says Mary Ann dejectedly. "Could there be something seriously wrong with him?"

Further questioning revealed that Jason had a history of ear infections. His ears had been almost constantly infected over the past several months, although they had cleared up each time with antibiotic treatment prescribed by a pediatrician. Had Mary Ann noticed Jason's having any trouble hearing? "No, he hears very well," she insists. "If anything, he's especially sensitive to noise. He gets very upset when we have big groups of friends and relatives over to our house."

Actually, Jason's symptoms are fairly common among children with some hearing impairment. His erratic and unorganized behavior, his frenetic activity, and even his heightened sensitivity to noisy environments are all consistent with some hearing loss. A child who is having difficulty hearing finds it hard to rely on an adult's help in focusing on particular activities the way toddlers and preschoolers usually do: if his mother suggests, "Would you like to sit at the table and color?" he may continue to dart around the room because he simply has not heard her. Furthermore, it is not uncommon for ear infections to result in some degree of hearing impairment. Mary Ann is advised to have Jason's hearing evaluated by a pediatric nose, ear and throat specialist.

The diagnosis? Jason is not hearing normally. Even though his ear infections have cleared up, they have left him with a buildup of fluid in the middle ear which prevents his eardrums from vibrating as they should in response to different sounds. Although he can *hear*, he cannot *distinguish* between various speech sounds. Consequently, of course, he cannot reproduce these sounds. His strange-sounding vocalizations are just a reflection of the confused way the world sounds to him.

At this critical period in Jason's language development, the fluid problem might have led to long-term language difficulties. Now that it has been diagnosed, however, the pediatrician can restore Jason's hearing by inserting tiny tubes into the eardrums. These tubes allow excess fluid to drain properly so that the eardrums can function.

Jason's story has a happy ending. Returning to the child-development laboratory two months after the operation, Jason is a different child. He no longer rushes around the room but settles down to play with the dump truck and doll. And even in the short time since his last observation session, his language development has caught up to age level.

Undetected hearing problems like Jason's are a major source of language difficulties in young children. If your child has had frequent ear infections, she is especially vulnerable to hearing impairment. If she has a history of ear infections, or if you suspect hearing loss (see box), check with your pediatrician about having your child's hearing tested. Although some children take longer to recover from a hearing loss than Jason did, the medium- to long-term prospects for normal speech are extremely good.

Articulation Problems

Pronunciation errors, or "articulation problems," are the most common type of language problem among young children, and most clear up on their own. Nonetheless, keep in mind that if a child is three years old, her speech should be largely comprehensible to her parents, and patient strangers who are willing to listen carefully should be able to understand at least some of what she says. Many children substitute one sound for another, of course—*wabbit* for *rabbit*, and *bery* for *very*. Such substitutions are perfectly normal in children until kindergarten or first grade. Errors of sound *omission*, on the other hand, are of greater concern, as when the child says *'ookie* for *cookie* and *'ee* for *see*. If your child is making similar errors, or if she is three

How Is Your Child's Hearing?

Here are some simple ways you can check your child's hearing at home. Obviously, this is not a professional hearing test. If you do notice that your child's behavior is *not* consistent with that described for her age group, it is a good idea to have her hearing checked.

Birth to three months: Should startle at loud, abrupt sounds—the clatter of pots and pans, a clap, a loud sneeze.

Four to five months: Should turn toward the source of a sound. When you speak to her, for example, she should turn toward you. When she is eating, she should be temporarily distracted by the sound of a radio turned on or a person talking. She should also be interested in sound-producing toys such as rattles and squeaky rubber ducks.

Seven to ten months: Should begin canonical babbling ("dadada," "yayaya," etc.) and respond to own name.

Ten to fifteen months: Should begin to understand at least a few words. When you say, "Daddy," "kitty," "light," or the word for some other object to which she is frequently exposed, she should begin to understand.

Fifteen to eighteen months: Should be able to respond when asked to do something familiar, such as "Give Mommy the ball," or "Pick up your bottle." Should respond even when you speak in a whisper.

years old and her speech is very unclear and difficult to understand, it would be wise to consult with a speech pathologist. If her peers or teachers have difficulty understanding her, she may have difficulty relating to other children. And if the problem persists as she enters school and begins to learn to read, she may find it hard to make connections between spoken and written words.

Delayed Language

When is a child's language considered "delayed"? How soon can a parent tell? Among parents, teachers, and even pediatricians, there appears to be a widespread belief that a two-year-old who has not yet begun to speak "will talk when she's ready," as long as she appears normal in other ways. We have all heard stories about children who have not spoken a word until they were two and a half or even three, and then "suddenly spoke in paragraphs!" All too often, the pediatrician reassures parents that their child will simply "outgrow" her language delay.

Recent research by psychologist Leslie Rescorla and her colleagues at Bryn Mawr College, however, shows that such optimism about children who have not said a word by their second birthdays is unfounded. By their second birthdays, most children have vocabularies of at least fifty words and are able to produce at least a few two-word "sentences." Among those who have attained these two language milestones on the second birthday, further development usually continues nicely. Among children who do not attain those milestones, but who are developing normally otherwise (and whose language comprehension is age-appropriate), Dr. Rescorla found that about half will continue to have serious language delay at ages three or four, and some even at five. (The other half *do* eventually "outgrow" the language problem.)

Some of the two-year-olds with language lags, for example, will later have problems with word order and grammar. For one thing, they fail to learn the morphemes, or small bits of words, that carry important meanings, such as the plural -*s*, or the past tense -*ed*. And as their thoughts outstrip their grammatical skills, they begin to form long strings of words *minus* appropriate grammatical structure (e.g., "I need throw onto here and come down these steps and come down here.").

As these children become older, other problems may become apparent. They may continue to reverse pronouns and routinely have difficulty finding the word they are looking for, resorting instead to circumlocutions. Instead of saying "swimming pool," for example, the child may say, "the place where we go and jump in deep water." In her research, Dr. Rescorla found no less than ninety-five percent of two-year-olds with language delays to be *boys*. And in many cases, there was a history of language delay in the family.

In the case of serious language delay, early detection and treatment can increase a child's chances for improvement. If your child is *at least* twenty-four months old and does not have a vocabulary of at least *fifty* words and has produced *no* two-word sentences, you should consider having her evaluated by a speech and language pathologist. (If your child was born prematurely, wait until twenty-four months after the *due* date, not the birth date.) Your pediatrician may be able to recommend one in your area, and many hospitals and universities also have clinics for the treatment of speech and language disorders.

BIBLIOGRAPHY

Books for Adults

Butler, S. *The Way of All Flesh.* New York: Dodd, 1957.

Chess, S. and Thomas, A. *Know Your Child: An Authoritative Guide for Today's Parents.* New York: Basic Books, 1987.

Chuskovsky, K. *From Two to Five.* Berkeley: University of California Press, 1962.

Fraiberg, S. *The Magic Years: Understanding and Handling the Problems of Early Childhood.* New York: Charles Scribner's Sons, 1959.

Gardner, H. *Frames of Mind: The Theory of Multiple Intelligences.* New York: Basic Books, 1983.

Greenspan, S. and Thorndike, N. *First Feelings: Milestones in the Emotional Development of Your Baby and Child.* New York: Viking, 1985.

Kaye, K. *The Mental and Social Life of Babies.* Chicago: University of Chicago Press, 1982.

Stern, D. *The Interpersonal World of the Infant: A View From Psychoanalysis and Developmental Psychology.* 1985.

Books for Children

Brown, M. W. *Goodnight Moon.* New York: Harper and Row, 1947.

Hill, E. *Spot.* New York: Putnam, 1980.

Hill, E. *Spot's First Picnic.* Putnam, 1980.

Oxenbury, H. *Clap Hands.* New York: Aladdin Books, MacMillan, 1987.

Oxenbury, H. *Tickle, Tickle.* New York: Aladdin Books, MacMillan, 1987.

Oxenbury, H. *All Fall Down.* New York: Aladdin Books, MacMillan, 1987.

Sendak, M. *Where the Wild Things Are.* New York: Harper and Row, 1963.

Seuss, Dr. *Green Eggs and Ham.* New York: Beginner Books, Random House, 1960.

INDEX

Activities, language-enriching (boxed sidebars): for eight- to sixteen-month-olds, 91, 97, 98, 99, 101; for newborns, 35, 37, 38–41, 42; for sixteen- to twenty-four-month-olds, 114, 116, 120, 124, 125, 126, 130; for thirty- to thirty-six-month-olds, 174, 187, 189; for twenty-four- to thirty-month-olds, 147, 148, 150, 152, 156; for two- to eight-month-olds, 57, 59, 62, 66

Animism, 168

Articulation problems, 196, 200–202

Babies, eight to sixteen months old, 77–103; and goal-directed behavior, 82–84; helping with everyday language learning of, 95–100; language development of, 86–95; language-enriching activities for (boxed sidebars), 91, 97, 98, 99, 101; and motor skills, 80–82, 102; questions and answers concerning, 101–103; sociability of, 84–86; and social referencing, 85–86; *see also* Toddlers

Babies, newborn, 19–43; alertness of, 22–24; body language of, 33; and eye contact, 26–27; and facial expressions, 32–33;